Computer Systems Laboratory

for Raspberry Pi

Sean Lawless

Computer Systems Laboratory

for Raspberry Pi

Sean Lawless

This is a Leanpub book. Leanpub empowers authors and publishers with the Lean Publishing process. Lean Publishing is the act of publishing an in-progress ebook using lightweight tools and many iterations to get reader feedback, pivot until you have the right book and build traction once you do.

Contents

Lab 1: Raspberry Pi

1.0 Disclaimer

Raspberry Pi is a trademark of the Raspberry Pi Foundation. All attempts were made to comply with the Raspberry Pi Marks copyright agreement when using the name Raspberry Pi and the Raspberry Pi logo. Reference: https://www.raspberrypi.org/trademark-rules/

1.1 Why the Raspberry Pi?

The Raspberry Pi platform, or RPi for short, is unique in many ways. A low cost combined with video capabilities, it can become a viable development environment when running a Linux OS. At the same time, its simplicity and documentation make it ideal for systems engineering projects. All that is needed for a complete systems engineering experience is two Raspberry Pi's, one running a Linux OS and used to edit, create and debug the software that executes on a second RPi. The GPIO pin out is also very helpful, eliminating the need for any soldering or third party hardware in order to connect the two RPi's.

Not to be overlooked for the beginning systems software creator however, is the removable SD card that contains the binary image that the RPi will automatically execute upon start up. Having the boot image on a removable SD card greatly simplifies initial system engineering development. Those new to software development can take their time to build up to leaning how to move a compiled binary to another hardware system for execution. With the RPi it is possible to move the SD card to the PC used to create the executable binary and copy the file in a way familiar to most computer users. On RPi power up a file on the SD card is executed automatically. To execute our software creations, we rename the original file (Linux kernel) and copy our own creation with a matching name, and then power up the RPi to execute our creation. This makes the Raspberry Pi series of laboratory assignments the simplest for introductory students.

If not all of the previous discussion was understood, no worries. We will get to each in time. This chapter starts the journey by describing the details of RPi B+/2/3 hardware, identifying the CPU, RAM and peripherals as well as the external connections (USB ports, etc.). This is a general overview but by the end of this chapter the reader should know the names of the major peripherals on the motherboard as well as the locations of the RAM, CPU and peripheral connections.

All software created in this laboratory book, as well as in the companion main book, are available to the public at the authors GitHub page, https://github.com/sean-lawless/computersystems. This repository holds the latest source code, chapter by chapter, which are meant to be used to follow along with the chapters of this book.

1.2 Raspberry Pi Hardware

The Raspberry Pi 2/3 and B+ have mostly the same hardware except the CPU, GPU (Graphics Processing Unit) and RAM are upgraded in the RPi 2. The RPi 3 has a further upgraded CPU and RAM as well as a separate chip for WiFi and Bluetooth. Let us view a picture of the hardware now, with the majority of the peripherals named.

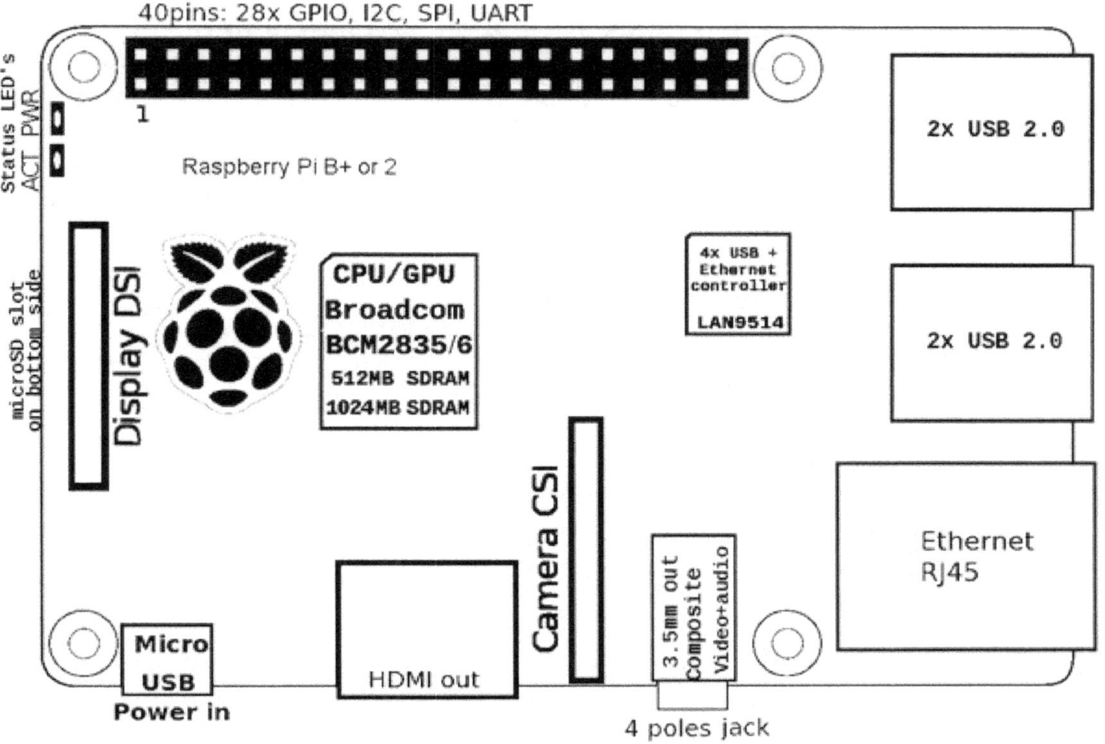

Fig 1: Raspberry Pi hardware

The core computer is contained within the CPU (Central Processing Unit), GPU (Graphics Processing Unit) and RAM (Random Access Memory) that is packaged as a single physical chip, known as a System on a Chip (SoC). The BCM2835 is the SoC for the RPi B+, the BCM2836 the SoC for the RPi 2, and the BCM2837 for the RPi 3. The power supply is a micro USB, allowing many USB chargers to power the RPi. Another important interface is the HDMI out, which can be connected to any monitor or TV with an HDMI in jack. Or the LCD display DSI port can be used with compatible LCD displays. The USB connections allow the user to add a keyboard and mouse and interact with the computer, and Ethernet connects to the Internet. An important connection to system engineering is the microSD slot on the left underside of the board. The microSD card slot must have a SD card connected containing a valid executable image (Linux kernel or otherwise) or no software will execute when the hardware is powered on. It is this SD card that we will copy our initial software creations onto in order to execute them.

The lab assignments incrementally build an understanding of the development process, not just the result. If questions arise, do not get distressed immediately but instead continue reading at least one chapter ahead. If the question still remains, reread and/or ask a knowledgeable peer, teacher or the Internet for more help. With incremental development, the next step often reinforces the understanding of the last.

This is a very concise introduction to systems engineering and the C language at the same time. They should both reinforce the other and to understand one requires understanding the other. However to the casual reader it will appear as if you have been thrown in the deep end of the pool. Remain calm with an open mind and you may surprise yourself to learn that it can be understood.

1.3 Protect the Pi

The next project is to protect the Raspberry Pi. If you have purchased or been provided a protective case, please follow the provided instructions for installing the Pi. For those with a bare system in a box, do not remove the board from the box until a case is available. It is simple enough to create a case out of cardboard, plastic or other sturdy material. This lab assignment is to use your imagination and create a case to protect your Pi, leaving holes to connect the USB, Ethernet, microSD and HDMI connections. It is important for the Pi hardware to be accessible as the case will need to be opened and expanded upon in the future as the reader advances chapters. Be sure to leave the RPi board in the static bag while measuring or sketching an outline of it.

The goal of this lab is to become creative and understand the case is for protection and style. Creating a case is empowering and adds individuality which increases the bond between the user and the computer. Drawing, painting and decorating are fun, but so is designing the case so that it keeps the board off the bottom for ventilation. For younger readers it may be appropriate to use stickers to decorate an existing case to avoid damaging the computer. The quickest solution is to use the box the RPI arrived and add elevating posts, snip open the ports and reinforce with tape.

Important

Adult supervision required. Do not paint or decorate the inside of the case as some paints and stickers, etc. are conductive and can short circuit the board. Never use metal, or even cardboard with a metallic surface, for the inside of the case. During initial operation, constantly observe and check the temperature of any new case that is flammable, such as cardboard or other organic material. Test how hot the RPi gets in the case and create airflow vents. Note that both sides of the motherboard require ventilation. Feet to lift the bottom of the motherboard above the bottom of the case is often required. Cut up sticky pads and use at the board corners, or design the case to keep the board up. A case that could hold the RPi up sideways often ventilates nicely.

Below is an outline for a box to be used as a Raspberry Pi case. This is an upgraded design for the RPi B+/2, based on by James Delgarno's original design for the RPi A/B models. The case can open and close with the tabs and slits. The following picture may not be the correct scale, please be sure to verify the dimensions before creating a case using this template for your Pi. Cardboard cereal boxes are an easy cardboard to work with. If you are so lucky, check if the inside of the cover of your book is a case design for the Raspberry Pi. If so, detach the cover carefully and follow the instructions within the outline.

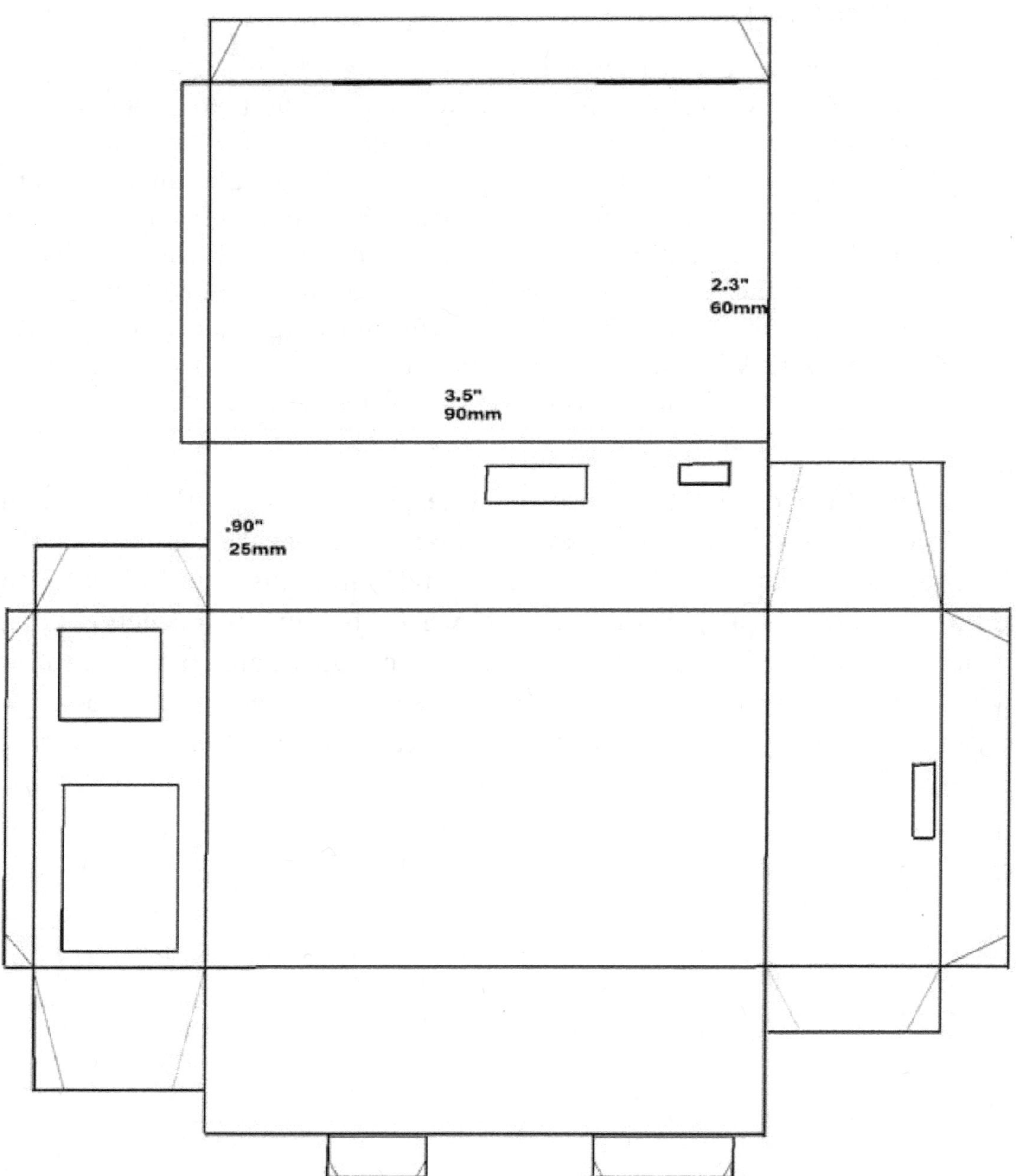

Fig 2: Raspberry Pi cardboard case

1.4 Connect the Pi

Practice performing the following sequence of actions with the board in its case and unpowered.

1. Connect and disconnect a USB keyboard to the Raspberry Pi.
2. Insert and remove microSD card into Raspberry Pi.
3. Connect and disconnect an Ethernet cable to the Raspberry Pi.
4. Connect and disconnect an HDMI cable to the Raspberry Pi.

All connectors must first be oriented before they will connect. User should identify the orientation of the connection on the board and orient the cable/connector before attempting connection. This process is expected to familiarize the user with the various connectors and their required orientation before connection. It may also require adding or adjusting holes in the case if homemade.

1.5 Create a Linux Installer

Important

Less experienced students should be provided preinstalled SD cards and skip this section or adults with prior experience can carefully direct and supervise.

To run Linux on the RPi we must first burn a Linux installer to the microSD card. It is recommended to install Raspbian, not NOOBs. Details change between releases so to keep this timeless, please just follow the installation directions on the raspberrypi.org website below. Windows PC users can use Win32DiskImager (or an equivalent utility) to burn the Raspbian distribution installer onto the SD card. For Linux OS users, consult the latest information on the Raspberry Pi website. In general though, download the installable image from the website and use the installation procedure to write the image to the microSD card connected to the PC with a USB adapter. Then insert the SD card into the RPi and it will install Linux on the next power up. See this link for burning an installer image to the microSD card to execute on the Raspberry Pi: https://www.raspberrypi.org/downloads/

1.6 Power the Pi

Time to power up the Raspberry Pi! Perform the following actions in order, starting with nothing connected.

Warning

Be sure to do them in this order as removing the microSD card while the board is powered on can corrupt the SD card.

1. Connect USB keyboard and mouse to the Raspberry Pi.
2. Insert microSD that was pre-installed with Raspbian.
3. Connect HDMI cable to Raspberry Pi and a Monitor or TV.
4. [OPTIONAL] Connect an Ethernet cable from Raspberry Pi to home router (Internet access).
5. Attach a 5 volt, 2 amp minimum USB charger, the USB end into the Raspberry Pi first, before plugging the other end into a power strip or outlet.

Important

If this lab involves children, adult supervision may be needed here regarding running Linux on the Raspberry Pi, especially with powering on and off. Be clear with the procedure and use power strips to make it easier to remove the microSD card only while the board is powered off.

The procedure above should power the board and start the Raspbian Linux operating system installer (or other image previously burned to the microSD card). If the SD card is empty or not properly imaged, the board will still have the red (power) LED lit. The yellow LED may flicker briefly when power is originally applied, this is good as it indicates the hardware found the startup files needed to perform pre-boot. After the Linux installer completes, the Raspbian OS will run and the next power up will start Linux directly. Do not power down yet until performing the shutdown procedure in the next section.

Important

For initial Raspberry Pi development where SD card removal is common, it is very helpful to use a power strip to turn the device on and off. If not, at least pull the plug from the wall instead of the USB connection. This is important to prevent wear on the USB power connection as well as the case (if cardboard).

1.7 The development system

Once Raspbian is installed, it should boot into a graphical interface. The user must open a system Terminal window to be able to enter commands. Linux variants differ on where to find this, but it can usually be found from the start menu, in system utilities or accessories. I find it helpful to create a shortcut to the Terminal on the desktop so I only have to find it once. On Raspbian the 'Terminal' is currently located in the top left 'Accessories' menu. Right click to add the 'Terminal' icon to the Desktop.

Opening the terminal, system shell, command prompt, etc. is the end of this chapter, but Linux will not be happy if we just turn off the power. Linux and other modern operating systems prefer that the user tell the operating system that it wishes to shut down. This is accomplished on Linux systems with the "shutdown" command. Enter the following command to shut down a Linux computer and attempt to power off hardware.

```
$ shutdown
```

If you see an error similar to 'Permission denied' you will need superuser privileges to use the 'shutdown' command. To execute, or 'do', a command as the 's'uper 'u'ser, enter 'sudo' before the command, like this example.

```
$ sudo shutdown
```

If Raspbian is installed then click the Shutdown... option in the upper left drop down start menu. Other graphical Linux systems typically have a shutdown option available from the start menu. If you cannot find it, the command line above will always works. Here is the new order for power cycling the Raspberry Pi as a development board.

Check connections of the Raspberry pi

1. Check USB keyboard, mouse and Ethernet connections to the Raspberry Pi.
2. Insert or check insertion of microSD installed with Raspbian Linux.
3. Check HDMI cable connection between the Raspberry Pi and Monitor.
4. Check attached 5 volt, 2 amp minimum USB charger at the USB end going into the Raspberry Pi.

Power on

1. Check or plug into power strip or wall outlet.
2. Turn on power strip (if present and off).
3. Linux OS will boot. Use Linux until shutdown is performed.

Power off

1. After ‘shutdown’ command, wait for all activity lights stop and monitor goes into power save mode indicating the Linux OS has completely shutdown.
2. Turn off power strip or unplug from wall outlet.

Lab 2: Command Shell and Editors

2.1 Why the Command Prompt or Shell?

This lab begins the discussion on how to create software for a computer system. These days there are a variety of graphical Integrated Development Environments, or IDEs, to choose from. However, these are often complex and can hide the details, requiring a large investment of time to configure and an incomplete understanding while using. To efficiently learn to create system software, the development environment should be step by step and easy to understand so that the process becomes comfortable and familiar. A familiar and repeatable process to create system software gives confidence to the developer.

Software development, especially system software, should be carefully created, one step at a time. Issuing commands in the command terminal will be explored as the first step in understanding the details of creating software. This knowledge can be directly applied to IDE configurations if/when the reader is ready to learn them.

The last laboratory assignment should have introduced the reader to the system terminal or command shell, which is historically the simplest form of development environment. This lab describes how to navigate file systems and use source code editors from the command shell. These skills are necessary to create the software in future laboratory assignments.

2.2 Exploring file systems from the command line

The command prompt on Unix and Windows systems allows the user to navigate the file system. A file system has a top down (hierarchical), structure and the term 'directory' is used to describe each layer. The top directory is the root of the file system.

Each directory contains files and other directories, with each directory containing more files and directories, on and on as desired. Upon opening the command shell the default directory is most often the users home directory.

The ‘pwd’ command can be used to display the complete path of the current working directory (‘pwd’ stand for Print Working Directory). The ‘pwd’ command, outputs the current file system path, or current working directory. The directory path is all the parent directories leading up to and including the current working directory. Every command prompt or system shell begins in a default location in the file system, usually the home directory for the user. Some Unix systems display the current working directory as part of the command prompt itself. Commands executed in the terminal use the current working directory when applying to or looking for files, etc.

To display the contents of a directory from the command prompt, the list directory, or ‘ls’, command can be used on Linux systems or the MinGW shell or PowerShell executing on Windows. More detailed information on the contents of a directory is available with the ‘ls -la’ command. In the output of ‘ls -la’ the files and directory names are displayed in the right column, while details of each is on the left. If the details on the far left begins with the letter ‘d’ then the name is associated with a directory, not a file.

The ‘ls’ command alone might have color coding to indicate directories vs. files and even executables, but not always. Linux, Mac and Windows based command terminals very in their user color friendliness, but ‘ls -la’ always works. Some commands available in the command shell usually provide information on usage if passed the ‘–help’ option. For example, more information about the list directory command can be viewed using ‘ls –help’.

Changing directories can be done with the ‘cd’ command. This command can take the user deeper into the file system hierarchy, or out of the file system entirely. For example, ‘cd source’ will move the current directory location one level down into the ‘source’ directory (if it exists in the current directory, or an error otherwise). To move down multiple directories with a single command add the ‘/’ character between the directories, for example ‘cd source/apps’. To move to an absolute path, start the path with the ‘/’ character, for example ‘cd /home/MyUserName’. To move up out of the current directory and into the parent of the current directory, the double dot notation is used, for example, the ‘cd ..’ command is used move up to the parent directory. To move back up the files system more than one level requires multiple or stacked double dots. For example, to move back two directories one should use the ‘cd ../..’ command.

Using the 'pwd', 'ls' and 'cd' commands allows one to navigate the directories of a file system of any depth.

It is best to create a specific location on the development system where the system software is created. The make directory command, or 'mkdir', creates a new directory within the existing directory. From the users home directory let us make a new 'source' directory with the 'mkdir source' command. This directory is where we can put the source code we are going to create. Then 'cd source' will move the command prompt into this directory. If lost, remember the 'pwd' command can be used to display the current directory.

2.3 Viewing and editing source code files

The simplest editor that can be used in the command line is 'pico'. This editor is very basic and simple, allowing users to view and edit text files such as C source code. The 'pico' interface is similar to other text editors. Use the arrow keys to move the cursor and add text wherever the cursor is located. The delete and backspace keys will remove a character in front of or behind the cursor. The 'pico' editor also accepts control characters to perform actions such as saving and exiting. All the commands supported are shown at the bottom of the editor. The ^ character indicates to hold the Ctrl key down while pressing the next character.

Knowing a few commands are required to use 'pico'. For example, to exit the editor requires holding down the Ctrl key and pressing X. This control sequence is commonly referred to as Ctrl-X or ^X. Ctrl-O writes Out the file, or saves it. To move text, there is Ctrl-K to cut text, and Ctrl-U to uncut text or paste. Ctrl-A or ^A brings up a menu of the commands, so Ctrl-A and then X exits the editor, similar to Ctrl-X. If you forget all other commands, remember Ctrl-A as that will bring up the menu of commands.

The cut and paste commands affect entire lines only but multiple lines can be combined, so three cuts and one uncut will paste three lines at the cursor location. This works great for moving and/or organizing the source code, but is a bit limited. Cut the lines, move the cursor to the new location and paste the lines to move blocks of source code. Let us use the 'pico' command line editor now to create the new file add.s.

```
$ pico add.s
```

Now it is time to write some ARM assembly code. Let us review the differences between the ARM assembly code representation of the pseudo code were learned and created in the companion book. Note that instead of the MOV instruction there is, 'ldr' and 'str', or load register and store register. Also, all the ARM assembly instructions are defined in lower case. For GCC assembler, comments follow any semicolon ampersand ';@'. Each line of code below is commented with information to aid in reading and understanding the assembly code.

```
ldr  r1,=Var1          ;@ load R1 register with address in RAM of Var1
ldr  r4, [r1]          ;@ load value of Var1 by referencing R1 address
add  r4, r4, #1        ;@ add one to the value
str  r4, [r1]          ;@ store the result to Var1 in RAM
```

The ARM **assembly** code above starts at the load register instruction 'ldr' and goes through to the store register instruction 'str'. To create the new file add.s, navigate to the directory where the file should be created ('source' folder) and type the command 'pico add.s'. Then enter the above ARM **assembly** into the new file add.s using the pico editor, pressing Ctrl-X and Enter to save the new file upon exit. This **assembly** language file creates a variable named 'Var1' and assigns it an initial value of zero (0).

2.4 Command line assembling

The command for **assembling assembly** files is called the **assembler** and can be invoked at the command line with the 'as' keyword followed by the name of the file to **assemble**. The **assembler** command 'as' requires options and therefore must be executed from the command prompt.

Important

For users developing on a PC (Windows or Linux), the examples for this chapter require a compiler for the ARM architecture be installed, not one for the x86 architecture commonly used for PCs. Please jump ahead to Section 3.2 and install the GCC tool set for ARM on the PC development system. Then replace the 'as' and 'objdump' commands below with the 'arm-none-eabi-as' and 'arm-none-eabi-objdump' commands respectfully for the remainder of this chapter. Raspbian users can use the default Linux assembler 'as' installed with Raspbian until it is replaced in Section 3.3.

Let us take a look at using the command 'as' to compile the file 'add.s', created in the last section.

```
$ as add.s
```

After executing this command with the assembly file named, the compiler creates a binary file named 'a.out'. You can see this new file if you use the 'ls' command to list the current directory contents. This 'a.out' file is not a very helpful name and things can get confusing quickly if compiling more than one assembly file. The '-o' option is available to the assembler that allows you to name the resulting output file. Here is the another example of compiling the 'add.s' file into the binary output file 'add.o'.

```
$ as add.s -o add.o
```

2.5 Command line disassemble

Once the assembly file is compiled into a binary output file, the object dump command, or 'objdump', can be used to read the binary executable and disassemble the contents back into human readable **assembly** language. Let us examine the recently compiled 'add.o' to understand what the **assembler** is doing in more detail.

{linenos=off,lang="bash"}} $ objdump -D add.o

```
add.o:     file format elf32-littlearm

Disassembly of section .text:

00000000 <.text>:
   0:   e59f1008        ldr     r1, [pc, #8]    ; 10 <.text+0x10>
   4:   e5914000        ldr     r4, [r1]
   8:   e2844001        add     r4, r4, #1
   c:   e5814000        str     r4, [r1]
  10:   00000000        andeq   r0, r0, r0

Disassembly of section .data:

00000000 <Var1>:
   0:   00000005        andeq   r0, r0, r0

Disassembly of section .ARM.attributes:

00000000 <.ARM.attributes>:
   0:   00001341        andeq   r1, r0, r1, asr #6
   4:   61656100        cmnvs   r5, r0, lsl #2
   8:   01006962        tsteq   r0, r2, ror #18
   c:   00000009        andeq   r0, r0, r9
  10:   01080106        tsteq   r8, r6, lsl #2arm
```

Note that the core of the .text section is close to what is in the 'add.s' so it appears the assembler is working correctly. Also note that a new .data section was created containing the variable 'Var1'.

Reviewing the dump of the binary above we see that while we did not declare the 'Var1' variable in the .s file, it was declared in the binary. To understand better why this is happening, let us add the variable declaration statement for 'Var1' to the original assembly source and recompile.

```
.section .data
Var1: .int 0            ;@ declare Var1 as an integer with value zero

.section .text
ldr  r1,=Var1           ;@ load R1 register with address in RAM of Var1
ldr  r4, [r1]           ;@ load value of Var1 by referencing R1 address
add  r4, r4, #1         ;@ add one to the value
str  r4, [r1]           ;@ store the result to Var1 in RAM
```

After compiling again, dump the object file again and note that the object dump files are identical. What is happening is that the assembler is being helpful by declaring the variable automatically as a integer type (.int) once used. This is helpful but can also lead to unintended consequences as all undefined variables will be declared as integer type and the initial value is not guaranteed. For clarity of reading the assembly as well as to ensure operation, it is best practice to always declare and initialize variables at the top of the .s file.

To summarize, the 'as' command **assembles** an **assembly** language file and creates a binary output file as a result, while the 'objdump' command **disassembles** a binary output file, showing the **assembly** language that the binary file represents. System software requires an accurate and reliable **assembler** to build a software binary correctly. A reliable and verified **assembler** is vital to the success of any software project. **Assembling** and dumping an **assembly** file is a good way to check what the **assembler** is doing. In the .text section of the 'objdump' output above is the assembly language the compiler created from 'add.s'. As expected, the binary generated by the assembler looks very similar to the assembly file we created to add one to a variable with a default value of zero. The reader is encouraged to modify the assembly language in 'add.s', recompile and examine the resulting changes with 'objdump'.

2.6 Assembly language branch instructions

The main branch assembly instructions for ARM CPU are branch 'b', branch less than or equal 'ble', and branch greater than 'bgt'. Labels are places in the assembly language where a branch instruction can jump to. Labels are defined in the GCC assembler as a single line containing the label name followed by a colon (:). Let us review the ARM specific assembly version of the generic assembly that was reviewed at the end of

Chapter 2. This assembly stores/loads the 'Count' variable value into a register and then loops, adding 1 to this register every loop. After every ten (10) times through the loop the value is saved back to the variable 'Count'. Remember that the '.section .data' is used to declare variables, and ';@' used to indicate a comment, in GCC assembly.

```
;@ Variables
.section .data
Count:                  ;@ declare Count as an Integer with value zero
.int 0

.section .text
ldr  r1,=Count          ;@ load R1 register with address in RAM of Count
ldr  r3, [r1]           ;@ load value of Var1 by referencing R1 address

_save:
str  r3, [r1]           ;@ store the result to Var1 in RAM
mov  r2, #1             ;@ initialize the save count to one

_loop:
add  r3, r3, #1         ;@ add one to the value
add  r2, r2, #1         ;@ add one to the save count
cmp  r2, #10            ;@ compare the store count
bgt  _save
b    _loop
```

2.7 Integer variable roll overs

Remember from Chapter 2 of the Computer System book that when an unsigned integer value increases beyond the maximum for the size of the variable, it rolls back to zero. For example, if an unsigned integer variable of size 32 bits and value 0xFFFFFFFF is increased by one, the value becomes 0x00000000. Modify the assembly language from the last section, adding a second variable to be increased by one only once 'Count' has reached its maximum value. So when increasing 'Count' by one, check if it results in a roll over to value zero (0). If so, 'Count2' should be incremented. To do this, initialize 'Count' and 'Count2' to zero and check 'Count' after every increment. If 'Count' is zero it rolled over so increment 'Count2' by one.

```
;@ Variables
.section .data
Count: .int 0           ;@ declare Count as Integer of value zero
Count2: .int 0          ;@ declare Count2 as Integer of value zero

.section .text
ldr  r1,=Count          ;@ load R1 register with address of Count
ldr  r2,=Count2         ;@ load R2 register with address of Count2

ldr  r3, [r1]           ;@ load Count1 value into R3 by referencing R1
_loop:
add  r3, r3, #1         ;@ add one to the value
str  r3, [r1]           ;@ store the result to Var1 in RAM
cmp  r3, #0             ;@ compare count to zero
ble  _rollover          ;@ branch to rollover if less or equal
b    _loop              ;@ branch to add one again to Count1
_rollover:
ldr  r3, [r1]           ;@ load Var1 into R3 by referencing R1
add  r3, r3, #1         ;@ add one to the value
str  r3, [r1]           ;@ store the result to Var1 in RAM
b    _loop              ;@ branch to add one again to Count1
```

Lab 3: GCC Tool Chain for ARM

3.1 Why GNU C for the Raspberry Pi?

The C programming language uses a **compiler** to create system software. It must create accurate and predictable software from the source code. The GNU C Compiler, or GCC, is a common compiler for building Linux systems as well as bare metal systems. Other C compilers are available but GCC is open source, integrated with the Linux OS, supports most CPU types and has cross compiler support for most major PC Operating Systems. The Raspberry Pi hardware is well supported by the GCC team and the ARM open source community in general.

3.2 Create a cross compiled executable

The command for compiling with GCC is 'gcc', while the command to link is 'ld'. However, on Linux development systems this default compiler and linker are designed for compiling Linux applications which can bring on a whole lot of dependencies and assumptions that are not valid for bare metal system software. Therefore the system engineer requires the 'arm-none-eabi-gcc' compiler instead of the default Linux GCC compiler installed by the OS. For a Linux development system, such as the Raspberry Pi running Raspbian, this version of the GCC compiler can be installed by issuing the 'sudo apt-get install gcc-arm-none-eabi' command with Internet access. This install includes the whole range of tools built specifically for bare metal ARM CPU compiling, for example 'arm-none-eabi-gcc', 'arm-none-eabi-as', 'arm-none-eabi-ld', 'arm-none-eabi-objdump', and 'arm-none-eabi-objcopy'. The different naming convention allows your Linux OS can keep the default compiler in place for building Linux applications.

```
$ sudo apt-get install gcc-arm-none-eabi
```

The 'arm-none-eabi-gcc' compiler and 'arm-none-eabi-ld' linker are designed for bare ARM systems without Linux. For Windows PC developers it is recommended to install

3rd party cross compiler tools for ARM. Presently, the GCC installer created by ARM Developer group at developer.arm.com is recommended for ARM cross compiler on Windows. Search online references for ARM cross compiling tools if you desire an alternative compiler or this information becomes out of date. Search for 'arm-none-eabi-gcc Windows download' for example. Presently for Windows a reliable and tested source can be found here 'https://developer.arm.com/tools-and-software/open-source-software/developer-tools/gnu-toolchain/gnu-rm/downloads'.

Information

If no online cross compiler is available for your OS, one can be built from the GCC source code. This is far from trivial however and beyond the scope of this introduction, but could be an option for those with more experience.

The newly installed compiler and linker commands can be executed from the command line, such as a Terminal in Linux or the Command Prompt in Windows. With the command line we can execute the compiler and linker commands, including options, to compile the file 'main.c' from Chapter 3 of the companion book. The example below compiles (executes arm-none-eabi-gcc at the command line) the file 'main.c' into main.o and then links (arm-none-eabi-ld) main.o into an Executable and Linkable Format (.elf) file. Finally the .elf is converted (arm-none-eabi-objcopy) into binary file led.bin which is then copied (cp or copy in Windows) to 'kernel.img', which is the name of the file the RPi automatically executes on power up.

Let us briefly review the options used with the GCC compiler. The '-c' is used to tell the compiler to compile and assemble the C source into an output file defined with the '-o', in the example below this would be 'main.o'. The remaining option is the '-I' option which tells the compiler which directory contains C header (.h) files #included within the C files. Option '-I.' tells the compiler to look in directory '.', which is the current directory. Here is an example of the steps entered into the Linux command shell to compile, link and prepare the binary executable.

```
$ arm-none-eabi-gcc -I. -o main.o main.c
$ arm-none-eabi-ld -o app.elf main.o
$ arm-none-eabi-objcopy app.elf -O binary app.bin
$ cp led.bin kernel.img
```

We will briefly mention the 'app.elf' linker file first to get it out of the way. Consider

ELF (.elf) files to be a form of formatted binary files, often required by 'objdump' and debuggers, but not directly executable by the CPU. It is important to understand that the linker (arm-none-eabi-ld) creates ELF files and this ELF is expected for object dump (arm-none-eabi-objdump) and debuggers such as GDB (see next chapter). The object copy (arm-none-eabi-objcopy), with '-O binary' option, can convert the ELF file into a raw executable binary file that can only then be directly executed. The last step of the sequence above copies (cp) this binary executable file to the 'kernel.img' file, which is the name needed for it to execute on the Raspberry Pi's Linux boot microSD card when powered on. The next step is to put this created 'kernel.img' file onto the microSD card and execute it.

3.3 Execute a binary on the Raspberry Pi

The last step before testing is to move the binary executable kernel.img to the boot file system. For the RPi, this is the file named kernel.img (or kernel7.img for RPi 2/3) in the root directory of the boot sector of the microSD card. Using a USB to microSD card adapter, move the microSD card to the development PC and then move/rename the existing Linux kernel (named above) to a new file, such as kernel_linux.img. If using a Linux system with automount, such as Raspbian, two folder partitions 'boot' and 'root' will be discovered and pop up when the USB adapter with microSD card is connected. The 'kernel.img' that the RPi executes at power on is in the 'boot' drive folder.

The Linux kernel we previously named kernel_linux.img will need to be renamed to kernel.img (or kernel7.img if RPi 2/3) before Linux will boot again. It is important to have a PC or other device available which can access the microSD card after this change in order to rename the Linux kernel back to kernel.img, otherwise the RPi cannot boot back into Linux. Whatever is in kernel.img the RPi will execute every boot. In a group environment will all RPi's, keep one system running Raspbian dedicated to this so no one has to wait for an available system.

The command sequence below will first save the Linux kernel and then copy the bare metal program we created and run it. Afterward, commands are shown to restore the Linux kernel and boot back into Linux on the RPi. The Raspberry Pi running Linux is using the same /boot folder and the Linux kernel was renamed and replaced with the bare metal image. After executing our creation it is required to delete or rename our creation and rename the Linux kernel back to kernel.img (or kernel7.img for RPi 2/3) before the RPi can boot into Linux again.

Warning

Only after renaming or backing up the real Linux kernel should you copy the newly compiled bare metal program into the root directory of the 'boot' driver of the microSD card to replace it. A second PC is required to restore the name the Linux kernel back to 'kernel.img' in order to boot into Linux again on the RPi.

The sequence below is for those developing and testing on the same RPi, while using another PC running a Linux OS to recover the Linux kernel of the RPI afterward on the microSD.

```
[AFTER COMPILING ON DEVELOPMENT RPI RUNNING LINUX]
$ mv /boot/kernel.img /boot/kernel_linux.img
$ cp kernel.img /boot/kernel.img
$ shutdown -h now
[POWER OFF]
[POWER ON]
<* Bare Metal Executable runs *>
[POWER OFF]
[PHYSICALLY REMOVE SD AND PLUG INTO SECOND LINUX PC]
$ sudo mount -t vfat /dev/sda1 /mnt/usb
$ mv /mnt/usb/kernel.img /mnt/usb/kernel_app.img
$ mv /mnt/usb/kernel_linux.img /mnt/usb/kernel.img
$ sudo umount /mnt/usb
[MOVE SD BACK TO RPI]
[POWER ON]
$
```

The sequence below is for those developing and testing on the same RPi while using another PC running a Windows OS to recover the Linux kernel of the RPI afterward on the microSD.

```
[AFTER COMPILING ON DEVELOPMENT RPI RUNNING LINUX]
$ mv /boot/kernel.img /boot/kernel_linux.img
$ cp kernel.img /boot/kernel.img
$ shutdown -h now
[POWER OFF]
[POWER ON]
<* Bare Metal Executable runs *>
[POWER OFF]
[PHYSICALLY REMOVE SD AND PLUG INTO WINDOWS PC AS DRIVE E:]
$ mv e:\kernel.img e:\kernel_app.img
$ mv e:\kernel_linux.img e:\kernel.img
[MOVE SD BACK TO RPI]
[POWER ON]
$
```

3.4 Cross compiler development PC

After Chapter 5 it will no longer be possible to use the same RPi system for development as well as to execute the compiled system software. The system software will soon open a physical communications channel with the development system, so both a development PC and an RPi are required. This development PC is used to edit, compile and distribute the software and to communicate with the RPi during system software execution. It is recommended to use two RPi's, with one system running Raspbian Linux as the development system and the other running the bare metal application and communicating with the RPi system under development. Windows, Linux or MacOS can be used as the development system. All that is needed is a compatible USB to micro SD card adapter, USB TTL (see chapter 6), source file editor, command shell and the correct 'arm-none-eabi' cross compiler installed on the OS being used as the development system.

Shutting down Linux in order to test a bare metal application, and then restoring the Linux kernel on the SD card, can quickly test ones patience. To become more efficient with this process requires we transition to compiling for the RPi with a cross compiler on a separate development PC. The USB adapter to the SD card can be used to copy the compiled image that we wish to execute on the RPi. Here is a command line example of mounting and copying to a USB device. This overwrites the existing kernel.img, assuming it was not the linux kernel but the last test. This type of procedure is common when the microSD card is dedicated to the RPi used for testing, and the Linux kernel has already been archived and or renamed.

```
$ ls /dev/sd*
[INSERT USB TO SD CARD ADAPTER]
$ ls /dev/sd*
[THE SD ADAPTER IS THE NEW ONE]
[EXAMPLE BELOW USES /dev/sda1 CHANGE WITH ABOVE IF DIFFERENT]
$ sudo mount -t vfat /dev/sda1 /mnt/usb
$ cp kernel.img /mnt/usb/kernel.img
$ sudo umount /mnt/usb
[REMOVE SD ADAPTER]
[MOVE SD ADAPTER TO SECOND TEST RPI]
[POWER ON SECOND TEST RPI]
<* Bare Metal Executable runs *>
[POWER OFF SECOND TEST RPI]
[REPEAT]
```

This example assumes '/mnt/usb' is a valid empty directory and the Linux system did not already automount the USB drive. With Raspbian and automount, the procedure to copy the file ultimately becomes one 'cp' line once the mount location is known. Below is the sequence of commands needed to build and copy the executable to the microSD card on a Linux OS with automount, for executing on the RPi. Optionally the the File Manager GUI application can be used to rename and copy and paste the kernel.img file to the mounted /boot folder.

```
$ arm-none-eabi-gcc -I. -o main.o main.c
$ arm-none-eabi-ld -o app.elf main.o
$ arm-none-eabi-objcopy app.elf -O binary app.bin
$ cp app.bin kernel.img
[INSERT USB TO SD CARD ADAPTER]
$ cp kernel.img /mnt/usb/boot/kernel.img
[MOVE SD ADAPTER TO SECOND TEST RPI]
[POWER ON SECOND TEST RPI]
<* Bare Metal Executable runs *>
[POWER OFF SECOND TEST RPI]
[MOVE SD CARD OF TEST RPI TO USB ADAPTER]
[REPEAT]
```

On Windows systems with an 'arm-none-eabi' cross compiler installed, the same sequence of commands, including options, are needed to compile the file 'main.c', link 'main.o' into an Executable and Linkable Format (.elf) file and finally into the binary files 'led.bin' and 'kernel.img'. However, Windows automount will activate a new drive letter, for example drive E: for the SD card 'boot' partition.

```
[MOVE SD TO PC, E: DRIVE]
$ cp kernel.img e:\kernel.img
[DISCONNECT SD/USB IN OS]
[MOVE SD BACK TO RPI]
[POWER ON]
<* Program runs *>
[POWER OFF]
[REPEAT]
```

With a Linux OS supporting automount (Raspbian, etc.), or Windows, the folders of the SD card open upon connecting the USB device. An alternate procedure to those above is to drag and drop, or copy and paste, the 'kernel.img' from the location where it was created and onto the connected boot drive. On Windows there is only one drive letter that is accessible when the USB adapter is plugged in so copy the kernel.img file to the root directory of that drive. If Raspbian was previously installed on the microSD card there will be two drives that open when USB is connected. Copy the 'kernel.img' file to the 'boot' drive.

3.5 Consistent cross compiler development

To compile, link and execute a program requires fewer steps when using a dedicated development PC. This cross compiling on a fast development PC will be used in all the examples going forward. Using two RPi's, one for the development Linux OS and the other for the system under test, is the recommended option. What is needed now is a simpler way to build the software. The majority of steps in the previous section were to compile and link the software.

To aid ease of use and ensure repeatability in the compilation and linking process it is recommended to use a build script. The shell commands can be stored and executed one at a time in sequence using a simple file. Create a file named 'build.sh' (or 'build.bat' if Windows) and put the compilation and linking commands above in it, one command per line. Then to compile, instead of typing each line, enter a single command at the command prompt to execute the script './build.sh' (or '.\build.bat' for Windows).

```
$ ./build.sh
arm-none-eabi-gcc -c -I. -o main.o main.c
arm-none-eabi-ld -o app.elf main.o
arm-none-eabi-objcopy app.elf -O binary app.bin
```

The build script is vital to creating system software in a consistent and repeatable way. If you see a 'permission denied' error on Linux it is because the file is not executable. The 'chmod +x build.sh' command will make the 'build.sh' file executable.

3.6 Compile and link executable for bare metal

Using the cross compiler on the development system, we first compile the file 'main.c', then link main.o into an '.elf' file and finally into the binary files 'app.bin' and 'kernel.img'. Let us expand upon the 'build.sh' from last section and introduce some options to the GCC compiler so that it will create a more targeted and optimized executable. One feature we will use is the '-O', or optimize, option. There are different types of optimizations available for '-O' option. Option '-O0' indicates to the compiler to not optimize at all and this is helpful for debugging or reviewing the resulting assembly language. Option '-Os' tells the compiler to optimize for size, creating the smallest binary possible from the source code. Option '-O2' tells the compiler to optimize for a combination of size and speed and is the option recommended.

The option '-ffreestanding' tells the compiler that the compiled binary is free standing and will not be running on Linux or using the GCC standard library, or stdlib, which is normally linked automatically when creating a binary. The freestanding option creates what is known as a 'bare metal' executable that will be completely independent of any other software. The '-ffreestanding' option tells the compiler not to create the default _start assembly entry point to the software. With this option it is required to put main.c first in the link order so that main() will be the entry point.

```
arm-none-eabi-gcc -c -O2 -ffreestanding -I. -o main.o main.c
arm-none-eabi-ld -o app.elf main.o
arm-none-eabi-objcopy app.elf -O binary app.bin
cp app.bin kernel.img
```

To review, executing this program requires overwriting the kernel.img on the microSD card. Here is the sequence events again when using a Windows PC for development.

```
[MOVE SD TO PC E: DRIVE]
$ cp e:\kernel.img e:\kernel_last.img
$ cp app.bin e:\kernel.img
[DISCONNECT SD/USB IN OS]
[MOVE SD BACK TO RPI]
[POWER ON]
<* Program runs *>
```

Using the example source code and procedure, test that the application will execute the loop and run forever. Run this application and compare the LED status with powering on the RPi without a microSD card present. By viewing the LED during application execution, how can you tell the difference between the application execution and running the RPi without an SD card? Were you able to verify that the software binary executes the loop forever? Change the source to loop a million times and then exit main. If you recompile and test, does the LED behave differently? Depending on the version of RPi you are executing on, your observations may vary. One piece of the puzzle is still missing.

Let us update our 'build.sh' now, using a script comment (#) to add comments on how to configure. The example below assumes you are building for the RPi B+ but this can be changed by changing the '-DRPI=' value to the number version of your RPi; 1, 2, 3 or 4.

```
#options -ffreestanding ensures no linkage to GCC external libraries
#option -c compiles/assembles, -O2 optimizes, -ggdb adds debug symbols

#Compile main.c for RPI 1 with debug symbols and no optimizations
arm-none-eabi-gcc -c -DRPI=1 -O0 -ffreestanding -I. -o main.o main.c

#Use ld to link with RPi memory map
arm-none-eabi-ld -T memory.map -o app.elf main.o

#strip elf into binary and copy to kernel.img
arm-none-eabi-objcopy app.elf -O binary app.bin
cp app.bin kernel.img
```

Information

DEPRECATED. The following is historic and not necessary for current versions of GCC. The CPU specific options below can be enabled to allow the compiler to do CPU specific optimizations in conjunction with -O2 and -Os options.

The GCC compiler, including 'arm-none-eabi-gcc', have compile options that will generate assembly code correctly for specific ARM CPU's. For the RPi, these changes are different depending on whether the hardware is an RPi B+, RPi 2, 3 or 4. For the RPi B+, add the option '-mcpu=arm1176jzf-s' to the 'arm-none-eabi-gcc' compiler. For the RPi 2, add the options '-march=armv7-a' and '-mtune=cortex-a7' to create an executable specific to the RPi 2 CPU. For the RPI 3 the options are '-march=armv8-a+crc' and '-mtune=cortex-a53' for the 64 bit 4 core ARM Cortex A53 CPU within the SoC.

Now the application should build and execute specifically for the RPi hardware you have. However, with the simple application we created there is no way know if the software executes correctly. In the next chapter we will enable the activity LED on the RPi so we can physically see our software in action.

Lab 4: GPIO and LED

4.1 Why the GPIO and LED?

Using a GPIO interface to enable an LED is often the simplest system engineering challenge that will result in a physical change visible to the user. While the RPi has an onboard LED that is connected to the GPIO interface, it is the same software procedure to turn on or off any of the RPI GPIOs if they were connected to an external LED. GPIOs can connect to LEDs, motors or other electronics and/or a separate breadboard connected to one or more external electrical circuits. The internal activity LED (the yellow one) is connected and controlled by the RPi GPIO number 47 (for RPI B+ through 2, the RPI 3 B+ uses GPIO 29 and RPI 4 uses GPIO 42).

With some carefully written lines of code it should be possible to turn the GPIO on or off, changing the status of the onboard LED so as to be visible to the user. Those wishing to use external electronics with the Raspberry Pi must take note that the GPIO signals use 3.3V, which is not compatible with 5V peripherals, such as some motors, etc. The RPi GPIO pins should never be connected to 5V inputs without a proper voltage divider to achieve 3.3V. Failure to follow this warning will destroy your RPi. An RPi with GPIO connected to a 5V output has undefined behavior and can also damage the RPi (although maybe not with as much certainty as an input).

The previous laboratory procedures have built up the experience needed for the reader to now write system software that performs a visible change to the hardware. Let us carefully understand the remainder of this laboratory procedure. Concepts missed or misunderstood now can lead to confusion going forward, however do not let yourself get hung up on any one issue before continuing as major concepts are further clarified in future chapters.

4.2 Raspberry Pi memory map

The RPI hardware has a fixed location memory map configuration for peripherals. The interface to the RPi B+ memory map for the peripheral registers begins at address

0x20000000, at the top of the memory map. At this address begins the peripherals that can be accessed directly by software. The RPi 2 and 3 peripherals begin at address 0x3F000000 in the memory map. The RPi 4 has more RAM so the peripheral registers do not begin until address 0xFE000000. Here is a picture of the RPi B+ hardware memory map showing a software program loaded for execution at address 0x00008000 to 0x01000000. In this picture the alternate peripheral register begin address of 0xE0000000 is defined, but this location is no longer used and 0x20000000 should be used instead.

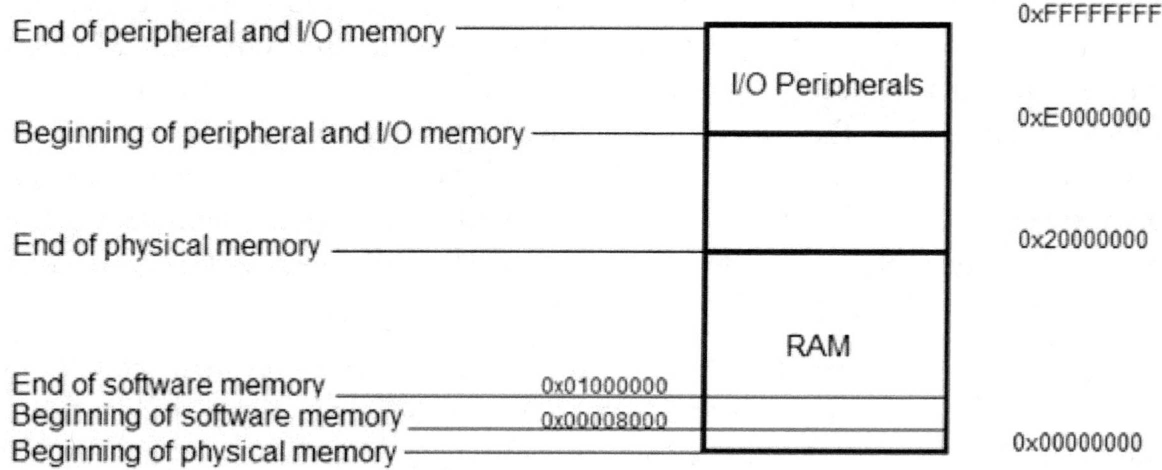

Fig 3: Raspberry Pi hardware memory map

Before writing any code let us review the memory map file 'memory.map' created in the the main book. For the RPi we must make a small modification to the linker script 'memory.map' created in Chapter 4 of the companion book. Since the RPi, upon boot up, expects to execute a Linux kernel, and a Linux kernel typically begins execution at address 0x8000 (for various reasons), we must modify the ORIGIN field to reflect this. Please modify the 'memory.map' file at this time, setting the ORIGIN to 0x8000.

```
MEMORY
{
    ram : ORIGIN = 0x8000, LENGTH = 0x1000000
}
```

We also need to change the build script to use this memory map. Open the 'build.sh/build.bat' file created at the end of chapter 3 and change the linking command to use the memory map.

```
#Use ld to link with RPi memory map
arm-none-eabi-ld -T memory.map -o app.elf main.o ..\..\boards\rpi\boar\
d.o
```

It would also be advisable, although not required, to change the name of the application from 'app' to 'led', as the application we are going to create in this chapter will active the LED.

4.3 Create/Edit board.h definitions file

To put the system software together, let us start by using the definitions in the system.h header file created and updated in this same chapter of the main book. First we should define the specific RPi register addresses from the memory map so they are easy to read and understand when writing and reading the source code. These register address definitions are board specific, so let use create a new file name 'board.h' and define them now. For reference, the peripheral base addresses described above, defined as RPI_BASE below, is documented at the following link: https://www.raspberrypi.org/documentation/hardware/raspberrypi/ peripheral_addresses.md

The GPIO register offsets are defined in Chapter 6 of the RPi hardware documentation file, BMC2835-ARM-Peripheral.pdf. Note that the documentation for this chapter uses addresses starting at 0x7E000000, yet neither the code or the link above uses this address. It should be stated that the BCM2835 documentation has many errors and out of date sections, but it is the best the RPi community has.

The following are the initial definitions defined to use the RPI_BASE define, so that they one change can allow the code to be used for various versions of the RPi. These source code definitions use the Field Name's in the documentation, for example, GPIO set register 0 is defined in Chapter 6, and below, as GPSET0. This should make looking up register names in the documentation simpler. For now we are only interested in the Pin Output Set, Pin Output Clear and GPIO Pin Pull-up/down Enable registers. Let use create and review this board.h file now, based on the documentation.

```
/*......................................................................*/
/* Configuration                                                        */
/*......................................................................*/
/*
 * Base of peripheral memory map
*/
#if RPI == 1
#define RPI_BASE          0x20000000  /* RPi B+ */
#elif RPI == 4
#define RPI_BASE          0xFE000000 /* RPi 4 */
#else
#define RPI_BASE          0x3F000000  /* RPi 2/3 */
#endif

/*
 * GPIO SET, CLEAR and PULL UP/DOWN ENABLE register addresses
*/
#define GPSET0           (RPI_BASE | 0x0020001C)
#define GPSET1           (RPI_BASE | 0x00200020)
#define GPCLR0           (RPI_BASE | 0x00200028)
#define GPCLR1           (RPI_BASE | 0x0020002C)
#define GPPUD            (RPI_BASE | 0x00200094)
#define GPPUDCLK0        (RPI_BASE | 0x00200098)
#define GPPUDCLK1        (RPI_BASE | 0x0020009C)
```

Be sure to use the correct RPI_BASE definition for the specific RPi being used to execute the created software. For example, if compiling this system software for the RPi B+, add the -DRPI=1 compiler options to the correct value from the header file will be used. The -D (define) option to GCC is used to define hardware type to compile the executable for. Below is an updated build.sh file that uses the -DRPI=1 option to compile the LED executable for RPi 1 B+ hardware. If using different RPI hardware, change the -DRPI= value.

```
#options -ffreestanding ensures no linkage to GCC external libraries
#option -c compiles/assembles, -O2 optimizes, -ggdb adds debug symbols

#Compile main.c for RPI 1 with debug symbols and no optimizations
#  change -DRPI to the version of RPI system used to execute
arm-none-eabi-gcc -c -DRPI=1 -ggdb -ffreestanding -I. -o main.o main.c
#Compile main.c for RPI 1 with no debug symbols and optimizations
#arm-none-eabi-gcc -c -DRPI=1 -O2 -ffreestanding -I. -o main.o main.c

#Use ld to link with RPi memory map
arm-none-eabi-ld -T memory.map -o led.elf main.o

#strip elf into binary and copy to kernel.img
arm-none-eabi-objcopy led.elf -O binary led.bin
cp led.bin kernel.img
```

4.4 Configuring the GPIO Pull up/down Enable register

The Raspberry Pi allows software to configure the GPIO type, and depending on this type the GPSET and GPCLR registers change the internal pull up or down switches differently. A GPSET will apply voltage to the GPIO and the GPCLR will remove voltage from the GPIO. How the voltage behaves depends on the configuration of the GPIO and whether a pull up or pull down resistor is present. Review the BCM2835 documentation again, pages 102 and 103 and note the Pull column.

The GPIO Pull-up/down Register (GPPUD) configures the use of internal physical resistors for each GPIO, for example, pull up or pull down resistors. On page 101 of the BCM2835 document it describes the GPPUD, GPPUDCLKn and how to use them. Note that it is possible to configure pull up, pull down or none (disable pull up/down) for each GPIO. In general, if an RPi GPIO is being used as described on page 102 or 103, it is best to configure the GPIOs with the GPPUD and GPPUDCLKn to the state defined in the Pull column. If the GPIO is being repurposed for a different use then it can and most likely should be reconfigured. An LED is an output GPIO and we see from the documentation that it should be configure as Pull High, or as a pull up GPIO.

Let us review and add the code below to the top of main() in main.c. This codes uses the GPPUD and GPPUDCLK1 to configure GPIO 47 to pull up for the activity LED. The RPI 3 and RPI 4 GPIO configuration will be shown at the end but the principle is the same. The pull up resistor helps trap the voltage to keep the LED lit and without flutter, even if the voltage supplied to the GPIO line is not constant over time.

```
/*
** GPPUD can be 0 (disable pull up/down)
** (1 << 0) enable pull down (low)
** (1 << 1) enable pull up (high)
*/

/* Set pull up (high) for LED GPIO 47. */
REG32(GPPUD) = (1 << 1); /* bit one is pull up */

/* Loop to wait until GPPUD assignment persists. */
for (i = 0; i < TOGGLE_LOOP_CNT / 1000; ++i)
  select = REG32(GPPUD);

/* Assign GPPUD settings to GPIO 47 in GPPUDCLK1. */
REG32(GPPUDCLK1) = (1 << (47 - 32)); /* GPIO 47 */

/* Loop to wait until GPPUD clock assignment persists. */
for (i = 0; i < TOGGLE_LOOP_CNT / 1000; ++i)
  select = REG32(GPPUDCLK1);
```

4.5 Operating a GPIO with software on the RPi

GPIOs are CPU controlled electrical circuits that can be turned on (supplied voltage) or turned off (grounded) with software. A GPIO can be used to supply voltage (turn on) or ground (turn off) an LED or small motor. Software can turn a GPIO on or off with the GPSET and GPCLR registers. GPSET0 contains the bits to turn on (drive high or apply voltage) the first 32 GPIOs (0-31) while GPSET1 contains the bits to turn on the remaining 32 GPIOS (32 - 63). The same is true for the GPCLR0 and GPCLR1, except these turn off (drive low or ground) the GPIOs. Turn on (drive high) the 47th

GPIO by setting GPSET1 bit 15 to one, since 47 minus the 32 GPIOs used by GPSET1 results in bit 15. Hopefully this example clearly explains how GPSET1 and GPCLR1 service the GPIOs 32 through 63.

```
  /* Other RPIs have LED at GPIO 47, so set GPIO 47. */
  REG32(GPSET1) = 1 << (47 - 32);
```

Now let us review an example of how to turn on the LED (RPi 1 or 2) using the GPIO interface. For each GPIO there is a set and a clear register which uses one bit per GPIO to turn it on (GPSET) or off (GPCLR).

```
#include <system.h>
#include <board.h>

/*.....................................................................*/
/* Global Function Definitions                                         */
/*.....................................................................*/

/*.....................................................................*/
/*        main: Application Entry Point                                */
/*                                                                     */
/*      Returns: Exit error                                            */
/*.....................................................................*/
int main(void)
{
  unsigned int i, reg;

  /*
  ** GPPUD can be 0 (disable pull up/down)
  ** (1 << 0) enable pull down (low)
  ** (1 << 1) enable pull up (high)
  */

  /* Set pull up (high) for LED GPIO 47. */
  REG32(GPPUD) = (1 << 1);
```

```
    /* Loop to wait until GPPUD assignment persists. */
    for (i = 0; i < TOGGLE_LOOP_CNT / 1000; ++i)
      select = REG32(GPPUD);

    /* Assign GPPUD settings to GPIO 47. */
    REG32(GPPUDCLK1) = (1 << (47 - 32)); /* GPIO 47 */

    /* Read back GPPUDCLK1 in a loop to stall/hold the change above. */
    for (i = 0; i < TOGGLE_LOOP_CNT / 1000; ++i)
      reg = REG32(GPPUDCLK1);

    /* RPI 1 has LED at GPIO 47, so set GPIO 47. */
    REG32(GPSET1) = 1 << (47 - 32);

    return 0;
}
```

To turn the LED off, replace the code comment with "turn on LED" with this.

```
    /* RPI 1 has LED at GPIO 47, so clear GPIO 47. */
    REG32(GPCLR1) = 1 << (47 - 32);
```

If you build and execute the example above it may or may not work, depending the version of RPi hardware and even the version of the boot up software on the microSD card. There is still one piece of the puzzle missing to ensure it will always work for all RPi revisions and boot configurations.

4.6 Peripheral and GPIO sharing with Function Select

Many times a hardware system has more peripherals than can be made available within the hardware address space. In these cases, a level select is used. This means a register acts as a selector and when modified can select a different set of peripherals and/or GPIOs per level, allowing different hardware configurations of the GPIO pins. The level select interface is used by software to access different peripherals with software that all share the same hardware address space. There is typically a default level selected at power on and software needs to change the level select infrequently. On the RPi, these level select registers are referred to as GPio Function Select registers, or GPFSELn registers.

Let use review the GPIO alternate functions that can be configured with the function or level select registers. In BMC2835-ARM-Peripheral.pdf, page 102 and 103, is a nice table showing all the GPIOs and their six (6) different alternate functions for each GPIO. We know from the GPFSELn definition on page 91 of the BCM2835 documentation that each GPIO is represented in the function select registers as 3 bits each, or the integer value 0 through 7. On page 92 there is this breakdown of the 3 bits.

```
000 = GPIO Pin 9 is an input
001 = GPIO Pin 9 is an output
100 = GPIO Pin 9 takes alternate function 0
101 = GPIO Pin 9 takes alternate function 1
110 = GPIO Pin 9 takes alternate function 2
111 = GPIO Pin 9 takes alternate function 3
011 = GPIO Pin 9 takes alternate function 4
010 = GPIO Pin 9 takes alternate function 5
```

The RPi hardware defines/allocates each General Purpose Input Output (GPIO) line with three (3) configuration bits, so each 32 bit function select register holds the settings for up to ten (10) GPIOs (30 bits with 2 unused bits). To repeat, the 32 bit select register can contain settings for 32 / 3, or 10 GPIOs plus two unused bits. For example, on the RPi with five level select registers (GPFSEL0, GPFSEL1, GPFSEL2, GPFSEL3 and GPFSEL4) would be able to control up to 50 GPIO pins. To access the GPIO 22 configuration will require using the level select register two (GPFSEL2). GPFSEL2 starts with the configuration for GPIO 20 at bit 0, so the configuration for GPIO would starts at bit six (6 = 2 x 3). Let us add the function select registers to the 'board.h' file now, above the definition for GPSET0.

```
/*
 * Base of peripheral memory map
*/
#if RPI == 1
#define RPI_BASE         0x20000000 /* RPi B+ */
#else
#define RPI_BASE         0x3F000000 /* RPi 2/3 */
#endif
#define GPIO_BASE        (RPI_BASE | 0x200000)

// GPIO function select (GFSEL) registers have 3 bits per GPIO
#define GPFSEL0          (GPIO_BASE | 0x0) // GPIO select 0
#define GPFSEL1          (GPIO_BASE | 0x4) // GPIO select 1
#define GPFSEL2          (GPIO_BASE | 0x8) // GPIO select 2
#define GPFSEL3          (GPIO_BASE | 0xC) // GPIO select 3
#define GPFSEL4          (GPIO_BASE | 0x10)// GPIO select 4
#define   GPIO_INPUT          (0 << 0) // GPIO is input      (000)
#define   GPIO_OUTPUT         (1 << 0) // GPIO is output     (001)
#define   GPIO_ALT0           (4)      // GPIO is Alternate0 (100)
#define   GPIO_ALT1           (5)      // GPIO is Alternate1 (101)
#define   GPIO_ALT2           (6)      // GPIO is Alternate2 (110)
#define   GPIO_ALT3           (7)      // GPIO is Alternate3 (111)
#define   GPIO_ALT4           (3)      // GPIO is Alternate4 (011)
#define   GPIO_ALT5           (2)      // GPIO is Alternate5 (010)

// GPIO SET/CLEAR registers have 1 bit per GPIO
#define GPSET0           (GPIO_BASE | 0x1C) // set0 (GPIO 0 - 31)
#define GPSET1           (GPIO_BASE | 0x20) // set1 (GPIO 32 - 63)
#define GPCLR0           (GPIO_BASE | 0x28) // clear0 (GPIO 0 - 31)
#define GPCLR1           (GPIO_BASE | 0x2C) // clear1 (GPIO 32 - 63)

// GPIO Pull Up and Down Configuration registers
#define GPPUD            (GPIO_BASE | 0x94)
#define   GPPUD_OFF        (0 << 0)
#define   GPPUD_PULL_DOWN (1 << 0)
#define   GPPUD_PULL_UP    (1 << 1)
```

```
#define GPPUDCLK0          (GPIO_BASE | 0x98)
#define GPPUDCLK1          (GPIO_BASE | 0x9C)
```

To clarify, if GPIO's are numbered starting from 0, and select registers are numbered starting from 0, GPIO's 0 through 9 are in select register 0, or GPFSEL0. Then GPIO's 10 through 19 would be in select register 1 or GPFSEL1. Below is a C source code example of assigning the fourth level select register (GPFSEL4) to configure GPIO 47. With GPFSEL4 now defined to a valid address in the hardware memory map this will configure GPIO 47. Noting the definitions above, for value of the GPFSEL4 if configured for GPIO 47 to an output (GPIO_OUTPUT) is to set bit 0, or (1 << 0). Since GPIO 47 is a simple LED it should be configured as an 'output' GPIO.

Reminder

Do not directly use the "or equal" (|=) or "and equal" (&=) assignment operations with the REG32() macro.

```
/* Enable LED. 3 bits per GPIO so 10 GPIOs per select register. */
/* GPIO 47 is 7th register in GPFSEL4, so 7 * 3 bits or bit 21. */
select = REG32(GPFSEL4);

/* 3 bits per GPIO, input (0), output (1) and alternate select */
/* 0 through 5. */

/* Configure the LED (GPIO 47) starting at bit 21, as output (1). */
select |= (GPIO_OUTPUT << 21);
REG32(GPFSEL4) = select;
```

The above source code first copies or saves the value of the GPIO select register to the variable 'select'. Then 'select' is OR'ed with the value one (1) shifted twenty one (21) times (1 << 21). This second assignment exactly sets bit 21 high, leaving the rest of the variable 'select' the same. The expression (1 << 23) is equal to the binary number 1000000000000000000000, but is more understandable to the hardware documentation reader when represented as the above expression of bit offsets. The last statement uses the REG32() macro to assign the new value to the hardware register in the memory map.

Each GPIO has three bits used for control which can be assigned a value of 0 through 7. The previous example works great only if all 3 bits of this GPIO are already zero. To create reliable system software it is often required to first clear the bits in question, before assigning a new value. Remember that the C language allows various assignment operations, such as +=, -=, |= and &=. These operations can be used to replace repeating the assigned variable. So 'select += ' can replace 'select = select +'. Below is the improved solution, which first clears and then assigns the correct GPIO select to enable the LED at GPIO 47 as an 'output' GPIO.

```
/* Enable LED. 3 bits per GPIO so 10 GPIOs per select register. */
/* GPIO 47 is 7th register in GPFSEL4, so 7 * 3 bits or bit 21. */

/* Clear the 3 bit range (7) starting at bit 21 */
select = REG32(GPFSEL4);
select &= ~(7 << 21);

/* 3 bits per GPIO, input (0), output (1) and alternate select */
/* 0 through 5. */

/* Configure the LED (GPIO 47) starting at bit 21, as output (1). */
select |= (GPIO_OUTPUT << 21);
REG32(GPFSEL4) = select;
```

4.7 Turn on or off the LED

Remember this statement from last chapter, "when main() finishes, the program will end and the hardware will halt". This is probably not what we want if our intention is to turn on the LED and leave it on. For the examples below we can achieve a wait by looping to assign the level select over and over. This should do nothing practical except cause a wait in the application, as this level select for the GPIO is already assigned.

```
/*....................................................................*/
/*        main: Application Entry Point                               */
/*                                                                    */
/*     Returns: Exit error                                            */
/*....................................................................*/
int main(void)
{
  unsigned int i, select;

  /*
  ** Enable LED. 3 bits per GPIO so 10 GPIOs per select register.
  ** GPIO 47 is 7th register in GPFSEL4, so 7 * 3 bits or bit 21
  */

  /* Clear the 3 bit range (7) starting at bit 21 */
  select = REG32(GPFSEL4);
  select &= ~(7 << 21);

  /* 3 bits per GPIO, input (0), output (1) and alternate select
   * 0 through 5. */

  /* Configure the LED (GPIO 47) as an output (1) */
  select |= GPIO_OUTPUT << 21;
  REG32(GPFSEL4) = select;

  /*
  ** GPPUD can be 0 (disable pull up/down)
  ** (1 << 0) enable pull down (low)
  ** (1 << 1) enable pull up (high)
  */

  /* Set pull up (high) for LED GPIO 47. */
  REG32(GPPUD) = GPPUD_PULL_UP;

  /* Read back the GPFSEL4 in a loop to stall/hold the change above. */
  for (i = 0; i < 5000; ++i)
```

```
    reg = REG32(GPFSEL4);

  /* Assign GPPUD settings to GPIO 47. */
  REG32(GPPUDCLK1) = (1 << (47 - 32)); /* GPIO 47 */

  /* Read back GPFSEL4 in a loop to stall/hold the change above. */
  for (i = 0; i < 5000; ++i)
    reg = REG32(GPFSEL4);

  /* Set GPIO 47 to turn on LED. */
  REG32(GPSET1) = 1 << (47 - 32);

  /* Set GPIO 47 to turn off LED. */
//  REG32(GPCLR1) = 1 << (47 - 32);

  /* Loop forever assigning the select register (doing nothing). */
  for (;;)
    REG32(GPIO_SELECT4) = select;

  return 0;
}
```

Compile the source code below and compile, the application should turn on the LED and then wait forever. Change the source code to comment out turning on the LED and uncomment the code that turns the LED off. After a recompile the application should turn off the LED and wait forever when executed. Change the source to not wait after enabling the LED (remove the loop to assign the level select and the end), and return from main() right after turning on or off the LED. By carefully observing the LED immediately upon execution, can you tell during execution between the application that turns the LED on and exits vs. the one that turns off the LED?

4.8 Blinking LED

Using the previous examples, create an additional application that turns the LED on, loops for a while to pause, and then turns the LED off, looping again to pause. Surround this code with another loop to run forever to create an application that will blink the LED on and off. To do this correctly requires adjusting the loop count until the LED on and off patterns are visible. The specific values depend on the hardware and compiler and this exercise is to use trial and error to figure how many times to loop between LED toggles before the LED flashing is visible.

Do not be impatient during test execution as the TOGGLE_LOOP_CNT may be too large for the hardware, etc. For example, an LED that changes after 10 minutes (or 60) can be fine-tuned by lowering the TOGGLE_LOOP_CNT to blink every second or so. It is also important that the loops access a volatile hardware register, and return the value from main(), otherwise the compiler might optimize the loop away entirely if it determines the loop is not needed for the application.

Notice that this version is the final version for this chapter and contains code for all RPI versions 1, 2, 3 and 4 hardware. The difference between RPI's is the GPIO used for the LED. Reviewing the code and comparing the differences between 'RPI == 3' code is a good way to understand the GPIO interface. RPI 4 uses GPIO 42, RPI 3 uses GPIO 29 and the other RPI's use GPIO 47 for the activity LED. The configuration of the GPIO for pull up is the same regardless of the GPIO number used.

```
/*...................................................................*/
/* Configuration                                                     */
/*...................................................................*/
/*
 * Configure number of loops reading HW register to wait one second
*/
#define TOGGLE_LOOP_CNT  5000000 /* 5MHz is about 1 second on B+ */
                                 /* and -O2 compiler optimizations. */

/*...................................................................*/
/* Global Function Definitions                                       */
/*...................................................................*/

int main(void)
{
  unsigned int i, select;

#if RPI == 4
```

```
  /* GPIO 42 is 2nd register in GPFSEL4, so 2 * 3 bits or bit 6. */
  /* Clear the 3 bit range (7) starting at bit 6 */
  select = REG32(GPFSEL4);
  select &= ~(7 << 6);

  /* Configure the LED (GPIO 42) starting at bit 6, as output (1). */
  select |= (GPIO_OUTPUT << 6);
  REG32(GPFSEL4) = select;
#elif RPI == 3
  /*
  ** Enable LED. 3 bits per GPIO, so 10 GPIOs per select register means
  ** GPIO 29 is select register two number 9. 3 bits per GPIO so 9
  ** starts at bit 27.
  */

  /* Clear the 3 bit range (7) starting at bit 27 */
  select = REG32(GPFSEL2);
  select &= ~(7 << 27);

  /* 3 bits per GPIO, input (0), output (1) and alternate select */
  /* 0 through 5. */

  /* Configure the LED (GPIO 29) starting at bit 27, as output (1). */
  select |= (GPIO_OUTPUT << 27);
  REG32(GPFSEL2) = select;
#else
  /* Enable LED. 3 bits per GPIO so 10 GPIOs per select register. */
  /* GPIO 47 is 7th register in GPFSEL4, so 7 * 3 bits or bit 21. */

  /* Clear the 3 bit range (7) starting at bit 21 */
  select = REG32(GPFSEL4);
  select &= ~(7 << 21);

  /* 3 bits per GPIO, input (0), output (1) and alternate select */
  /* 0 through 5. */
```

```
  /* Configure the LED (GPIO 47) starting at bit 21, as output (1). */
  select |= (GPIO_OUTPUT << 21);
  REG32(GPFSEL4) = select;
#endif

  /* GPPUD - GPio Pin Up Down configuration */
  /*   (0) disable pull up and pull down to float the GPIO */
  /*   (1 << 0) enable pull down (low) */
  /*   (1 << 1) enable pull up (high) */

  /* Always pull up (high) for LEDs as they require voltage. */
  REG32(GPPUD) = GPPUD_PULL_UP;

  /* Loop to wait until GPPUD assignment persists. */
  for (i = 0; i < TOGGLE_LOOP_CNT / 1000; ++i)
    select = REG32(GPFSEL4);

#if RPI == 4
  /* Push GPPUD settings to GPPUDCLK1 GPIO 42. */
  REG32(GPPUDCLK1) = (1 << (42 - 32)); /* GPIO 42 */
#elif RPI == 3
  /* Push GPPUD settings to GPPUDCLK0 GPIO 29. */
  REG32(GPPUDCLK0) = (1 << 29); /* GPIO 29 */
#else
  /* Push GPPUD settings to GPPUDCLK1 GPIO 47. */
  REG32(GPPUDCLK1) = (1 << (47 - 32)); /* GPIO 47 */
#endif

  /* Loop to wait until GPPUD clock assignment persists. */
  for (i = 0; i < TOGGLE_LOOP_CNT / 1000; ++i)
    select = REG32(GPFSEL4);

  /* Loop turning the activity LED on and off. */
  for (;;)
  {
    /* Turn on the activity LED. */
```

```
#if RPI == 4
    /* RPI 4 has LED at GPIO 42, so set GPIO 42. */
    REG32(GPSET1) = 1 << (42 - 32);
#elif RPI == 3
    /* RPI 3 has LED at GPIO 29, so set GPIO 29. */
    REG32(GPSET0) = 1 << 29;
#else
    /* Other RPIs have LED at GPIO 47, so set GPIO 47. */
    REG32(GPSET1) = 1 << (47 - 32);
#endif

    // Loop to wait a bit
    for (i = 0; i < TOGGLE_LOOP_CNT; ++i) /* loop to pause LED on */
      select = REG32(GPFSEL4);

    /* Turn off the activity LED. */
#if RPI == 4
    /* RPI 4 has LED at GPIO 42, so clear GPIO 42. */
    REG32(GPCLR1) = 1 << (42 - 32);
#elif RPI == 3
    /* RPI 3 has LED at GPIO 29, so clear GPIO 29. */
    REG32(GPCLR0) = 1 << 29;
#else
    /* Other RPIs have LED at GPIO 47, so clear GPIO 47. */
    REG32(GPCLR1) = 1 << (47 - 32);
#endif

    // Loop to wait a bit
    for (i = 0; i < TOGGLE_LOOP_CNT; ++i) /* loop to pause LED off */
      select = REG32(GPFSEL4);
  }
  return select;
}
```

Compile and execute this code and the LED should blink on and off for the RPi executing the software. Note that the TOGGLE_LOOP_CNT defined above is for the

RPi B+ and that this loop count is used for the hold wait when configuring the GPIO pull up and pull down registers. Congratulations on your success! It was not easily earned but has laid the foundation for all things that follow.

4.9 GDB and OpenOCD

The GCC ecosystem has GDB (GNU De-Bugger) for **debugging** executables over a remote JTAG connection to the RPI. On PC development systems it is required to purchase, configure and use a JTAG controller that supports the RPI (ARM) hardware and Windows/Linux OS. JTAG controller configuration procedures are product specific and beyond the scope of this document. Tutorials exist that demonstrate JTAG debugging with the RPI using different off the shelf commercial JTAG compatible controllers. For Linux development PCs, especially for an RPI development PC running Raspbian, there is a unique solution that allows us to use OpenOCD and wire the GPIOs directly between the RPI's.

Regardless of the JTAG adapter and physical connection between the development PC and the **remote target** RPI, the development PC must have the bare metal (arm-none-eabi) version of GDB installed. On Linux this can be accomplished with the following command.

```
$ sudo apt-get install gdb-arm-none-eabi
```

OpenOCD, or the Open On-Chip Debugger, is an open source tool that supports JTAG and GDB. A BCM2835 GPIO JTAG bit bang driver was created that allows an RPI development PC to use the GPIOs on the RPI board to bit bang a JTAG controller. This effectively turns the development PC into a JTAG controller at the same time it runs Raspbian. This BCM2835 driver for OpenOCD is still in development but is functional enough to be highly recommended as it requires no additional hardware to purchase. The BCM2835 driver is not included in the OpenOCD official release but can be built into the project at compile time. The following procedure will download the OpenOCD source tree, configure it for the BCM2835 GPIO driver, build the OpenOCD software and then install it on the Raspbian development PC.

First, be sure your Raspbian development PC is up to date.

```
$ sudo apt-get update
$ sudo apt-get upgrade -y
$ sudo apt-get dist-upgrade -y
```

Next be sure the dependencies necessary to build OpenOCD are installed before using Git to clone OpenOCD and prepare it for building.

```
$ sudo apt-get install git autoconf libtool
$ sudo apt-get install pkg-config libusb-1.0-0 libusb-1.0-0-dev
$ git clone git://git.code.sf.net/p/openocd/code openocd
$ cd openocd
$ ./bootstrap
```

Now configure, make and install the OpenOCD software on the Raspbian development PC.

Information

The following instructions were tested and are known to work on an RPI development PC running Raspbian.

```
$ ./configure --enable-bcm2835gpio --enable-sysfsgpio
$ make
$ sudo make install
```

4.10 Wiring and Configuring JTAG

With the OpenOCD BCM2835 GPIO JTAG controller installed from the previous chapter, we next need to wire together the RPI development PC with the **remote system** RPI to enable debugging. The JTAG GPIOs on the RPI are defined beginning with ARM_ in Section 6.2 (page 102) of the BCM2835-ARM-Peripherals.pdf document. This page shows the complete GPIO map for the Raspberry Pi, including all the alternate functions. The JTAG pins are designated through alternate 4 (Alt 4) of GPIO 22 (ARM_TRST), 23 (ARM_RTCK), 24 (ARM_TDO), 25 (ARM_TCK), 26 (ARM_TDI) and 27 (ARM_TMS). These GPIOs map to pin numbers and the picture shows the all the connections between the two RPi's exposed pins. I the picture the development PC is on top while the **remote systems**, or target to be debugged, is on the bottom.

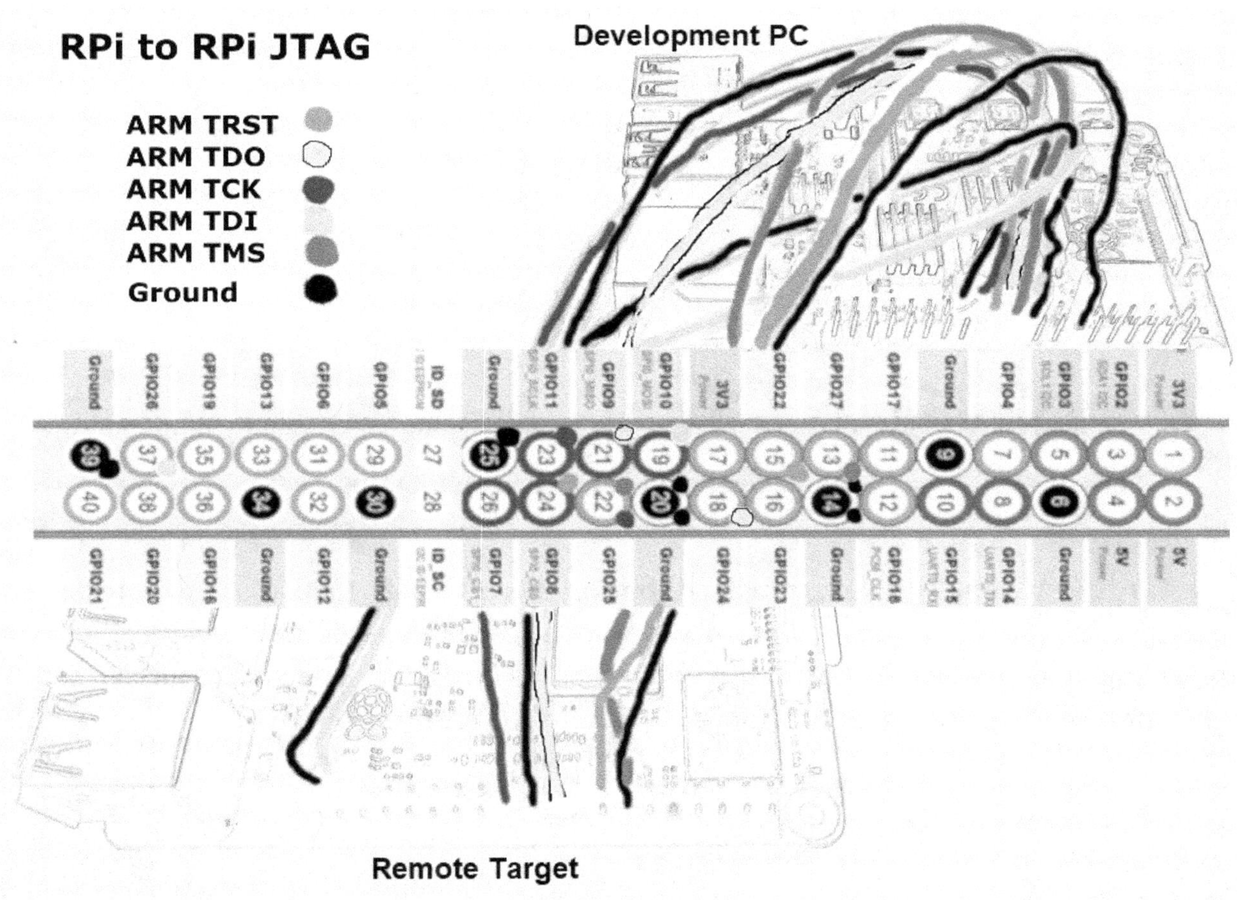

Fig 4: Raspberry Pi GPIO pinout

For the RPI development PC running Raspbian and using the OpenOCD bit bang JTAG controller, the default configuration file uses the following RPI GPIOs for the JTAG signals, GPIO 7 (ARM_TRST), ? (ARM_RTCK), 9 (ARM_TDO), 11 (ARM_TCK), 10 (ARM_TDI) and 25 (ARM_TMS). The following table shows the JTAG wiring between the RPI development PC (left) and the **remote target** RPI (right).

Fig 5: JTAG pin map for RPI development PC to RPI target

GPIO	Pin	Pin	GPIO	JTAG Signal	Color
7	24	15	22	ARM_TRST	Grey
?	?	16	23	ARM_RTCK*	-
9	21	18	24	ARM_TDO	Outline
11	23	22	25	ARM_TCK	Almost Black
10	19	37	26	ARM_TDI	Light Grey
25	22	13	27	ARM_TMS	Dark Grey
-	14	14	-	Ground	Black
-	20	39	-	Ground	Black
-	25	20	-	Ground	Black

Warning

Both RPIs should be powered down before connecting the JTAG GPIOs.

The **target system** software must configure these GPIOs to use select alternate 4 and then physically connect the GPIOs above to the development system PC. The following code needs to be added to main.c in order to select alternate four (4) operation of the GPIO pins to enable JTAG on the **remote system**.

```
/*
 * Enable the JTAG GPIOs
*/

/* Disable pull up/down for the next configured GPIO. */
REG32(GPPUD) = GPPUD_OFF;

/* Loop to wait until GPPUD assignment persists. */
for (i = 0; i < TOGGLE_LOOP_CNT / 1000; ++i)
  select = REG32(GPFSEL4);

// Apply to all the JTAG GPIO pins
REG32(GPPUDCLK0) = (1 << 22) | (1 << 23) | (1 << 24) | (1 << 25) |
                   (1 << 26) | (1 << 27);
```

```
/* Loop to wait until GPPUD clock assignment persists. */
for (i = 0; i < TOGGLE_LOOP_CNT / 1000; ++i)
  select = REG32(GPFSEL4);

// Select level alternate 4 to enable JTAG
select = REG32(GPFSEL2);
select &= ~(7 << 6); //gpio22
select |= GPIO_ALT4 << 6; //alt4 ARM_TRST
select &= ~(7 << 9); //gpio23
select |= GPIO_ALT4 << 9; //alt4 ARM_RTCK
select &= ~(7 << 12); //gpio24
select |= GPIO_ALT4 << 12; //alt4 ARM_TDO
select &= ~(7 << 15); //gpio25
select |= GPIO_ALT4 << 15; //alt4 ARM_TCK
select &= ~(7 << 18); //gpio26
select |= GPIO_ALT4 << 18; //alt4 ARM_TDI
select &= ~(7 << 21); //gpio27
select |= GPIO_ALT4 << 21; //alt4 ARM_TMS
REG32(GPFSEL2) = select;
```

Information

Some versions of RPI and boot code may interfere with the JTAG signals. To ensure the RPI boots with JTAG support edit the /boot/config.txt of the RPI executing the JTAG code above and add enable_jtag_gpio=1 to the end of the file.

Finally double check all the wiring and execute the created software on the **remote system** by copying the kernel.img file to the SD card boot folder as previously described in detail in Chapter 3. With the latest LED application executing and the JTAG wired to the **remote system**, it is now time to test the OpenOCD bit bang JTAG controller. Create file boards/rpi/openocd_rpi_jtag.cfg and add the following lines of configuration.

```
#
# Do not forget the ground connections
#

interface bcm2835gpio

bcm2835gpio_peripheral_base 0x3F000000

# RPI 2 (900 MHz clock)
bcm2835gpio_speed_coeffs 146203 36
# RPI 3 (1200 MHz clock)
#bcm2835gpio_speed_coeffs 194938 48

# Each of the JTAG lines need a gpio number set: tck tms tdi tdo
# RPI header pin numbers: 23 22 19 21
bcm2835gpio_jtag_nums 11 25 10 9

# RPI to RPI has trst pins only
bcm2835gpio_trst_num 7
reset_config trst_only trst_open_drain
#reset_config none
```

This configuration tells the OpenOCD driver the information it needs to control the JTAG signals on the GPIO lines that were previously connected. The final piece of the puzzle is to create the OpenOCD configuration file for the **remote system**. The following example is for the RPI 1, other configuration files exist in the companion files of the laboratory. Let us create boards/rpi/rpi1_jtag.cfg.

```
# Raspberry Pi 1

telnet_port 4444
gdb_port 3333

transport select jtag
adapter_khz 125
jtag_ntrst_delay 400

if { [info exists CHIPNAME] } {
   set  _CHIPNAME $CHIPNAME
} else {
   set  _CHIPNAME raspi
}

reset_config trst_only trst_open_drain
#reset_config none

if { [info exists CPU_TAPID ] } {
   set _CPU_TAPID $CPU_TAPID
} else {
   set _CPU_TAPID 0x07b7617F
}
jtag newtap $_CHIPNAME arm -irlen 5 -expected-id $_CPU_TAPID

set _TARGETNAME $_CHIPNAME.arm
target create $_TARGETNAME arm11 -chain-position $_TARGETNAME

$_TARGETNAME configure -event reset-assert-post { gdbinit }
$_TARGETNAME configure -event gdb-attach { halt }
```

Now execute OpenOCD, configuring it at run time with the two configuration files.

```
$ sudo openocd -f ./openocd_rpi_jtag.cfg -f ./rpi1_jtag.cfg
Open On-Chip Debugger 0.10.0+dev-00809-g7ee61869 (2019-05-11-00:02)
Licensed under GNU GPL v2
For bug reports, read
  http://openocd.org/doc/doxygen/bugs.html
BCM2835 GPIO: peripheral_base = 0x3f000000
BCM2835 GPIO: speed_coeffs = 146203, speed_offset = 36
BCM2835 GPIO config: tck = 11, tms = 25, tdi = 10, tdo = 9
BCM2835 GPIO config: trst = 7
trst_only separate trst_open_drain
adapter speed: 125 kHz
jtag_ntrst_delay: 400
trst_only separate trst_open_drain
Info : Listening on port 6666 for tcl connections
Info : Listening on port 4444 for telnet connections
Info : BCM2835 GPIO JTAG/SWD bitbang driver
Info : JTAG only mode enabled (specify swclk and swdio gpio to add SWD
Info : clock speed 125 kHz
Info : JTAG tap: raspi.arm tap/device found: 0x07b7617f (mfg: 0x0bf (Br
Info : found ARM1176
Info : raspi.arm: hardware has 6 breakpoints, 2 watchpoints
Info : Listening on port 3333 for gdb connections
```

If you see the output below, or something similar, congratulations you are now ready to debug with GDB. Leave this OpenOCD console running and open a new console window in Raspbian. In this new console let us install and execute GDB now.

```
$ sudo apt-get install gdb-arm-none-eabi
$ arm-none-eabi-gdb led.elf
GNU gdb (7.10-1+9) 7.10
Copyright (C) 2015 Free Software Foundation, Inc.
License GPLv3+: GNU GPL version 3 or later <http://gnu.org/licenses/gp
...
Reading symbols from ./led.elf...done.
(gdb)
```

Now at the GDB prompt, let us try the OpenOCD JTAG connection with the 'target remote' command.

```
(gdb) target remote localhost:3333
0x00008068 in ?? ()
(gdb)
```

If you see this it is great news. The final step is to recompile the LED application with debugging symbols in it. In build.sh add the -ggdb option to the list of options to arm-none-eabi-gcc command (arm-none-eabi-gcc -c -ggdb ...). This enables debug symbols so the code can be debugged. Now rebuild the LED and do the SD card dance to get the new software to execute again on the **remote system** RPI. OpenOCD in the other console should be spitting out errors once the **remote system** is power cycled. Ctl-C in the OpenOCD window to stop the program until the **remote system** is executing again and then issue the command to start OpenOCD again.

With the **remote system** now executing the latest software, and OpenOCD JTAG controller running successfully in another console window of the Raspbian development PC, let us retry GDB.

```
$ arm-none-eabi-gdb led.elf
...
Reading symbols from ./led.elf...done.
(gdb) target remote :3333
Remote debugging using :3333
main () at main.c:104
104     for (i = 0; i < TOGGLE_LOOP_CNT; ++i) /* loop to pause LED off
(gdb)
```

It would dramatically speed of the incremental build and test process if there was a way to load the executable without removing the SD card. It so happens that GDB can load ELF (.elf) files into system RAM for execution. We must first use GDB to connect over JTAG and stop execution of the current system software. Then we can issue the 'load led.elf' command. First, follow the previous instructions to open a new terminal and run OpenOCD on the development PC running Raspbian. Then build your application and open it with GDB, as below.

```
(gdb) load led.elf
Loading section .text, size 0x390 lma 0x8000
Start address 0x8000, load size 912
Transfer rate: 7296 bits in <1 sec, 912 bytes/write.
(gdb) continue
Continuing.
```

Now after ‘continuing’ in GDB, our newly created executable is running on the remote target. With this procedure we no longer need to swap out the SD card and copy the new kernel.img file to execute and test our new software creations. As long as the SD card is running in a loop and has enabled the JTAG GPIO’s to select alternate 4, GDB and OpenOCD can be used from the Raspbian development PC over the physical GPIO wires. For GDB to connect remember to use the ‘target remote’ command ((gdb) target remote :3333) and then load ((gbd) load led.elf) the new executable. Then the continue ((gdb) continue) command will execute the newly loaded executable.

If this is working congratulations. If not, recheck the connections and source code as JTAG is fickle. If everything is not perfect, nothing will work. The quality of wire has been shown to make a difference with JTAG and the speed can be increased with the OpenOCD adapter_khz setting if high quality wire and connectors are used.

Reminder

Some combinations of RPI and boot code may interfere with the JTAG GPIOs. To ensure the RPI boots with JTAG support edit the /boot/config.txt of the RPI executing the JTAG code above and add enable_jtag_gpio=1 to the end of the file.

4.11 Debugging with GDB

GDB supports an interactive Text User Interface, or TUI. Let us explore the ‘step’ and ‘breakpoint’ commands. The ‘step’ commands take no options and advances the execution to the next line of source code. The ‘break’ command takes a function name or file name with a colon ‘:’ and line number.

```
$ arm-none-eabi-gdb -tui led.elf
```

```
┌─main.c──────────────────────────────────────────────────────────────┐
|185                                                                  |
|186        /* Turn off the activity LED. */                          |
|187     #if RPI == 4                                                 |
|188        /* RPI 4 has LED at GPIO 42, so clear GPIO 42. */         |
|189        REG32(GPCLR1) = 1 << (42 - 32);                           |
|190     #elif RPI == 3                                               |
|191        /* RPI 3 has LED at GPIO 29, so clear GPIO 29. */         |
|192        REG32(GPCLR0) = 1 << 29;                                  |
|193     #else                                                        |
|194        /* Other RPIs have LED at GPIO 47, so clear GPIO 47. *|
|195        REG32(GPCLR1) = 1 << (47 - 32);                           |
|196     #endif                                                       |
|197                                                                  |
|198        // Loop to wait a bit                                      |
>|199        for (i = 0; i < TOGGLE_LOOP_CNT; ++i) /* loop to pause|
└─────────────────────────────────────────────────────────────────────┘
remote Remote target In: main                          L199   PC: 0x80cc
Reading symbols from led.elf...done.
(gdb) target remote :3333
Remote debugging using :3333
main () at main.c:200
(gdb) next
(gdb) break main.c:101
Breakpoint 1 at 0x8014: file main.c, line 101.
(gdb)
```

Stepping through our source code creations with a debugger and using **breakpoints** is a great way to reinforce our knowledge and build confidence in our emerging abilities as a systems software creator.

OpenOCD and GDB work better on some versions of RPI hardware than others. From the authors tests, the best RPI to use for a development PC is an RPI 2 or higher as these have multiple cores for Linux to utilize. The best RPI to use for the target system is an RPI B+ as it has full GDB support over OpenOCD. The RPI 2 as a target system could not be debugged with OpenOCD and GDB, while the RPI 3 B+ had limited debugging functionality. This appeared to be because OpenOCD does not completely support these versions of Cortex processors yet, or possibly because the GDB used with OpenOCD is dated. Specifically the development RPI running OpenOCD 0.10.0 and GDB 7.10 connecting ('target remote :3333') to the RPI 3 B+ target system would not 'step' or 'next' but would allow **break points** to be set. However, once a **break point** hit the stack and variables would be inaccessible until the user removed the **break points**, continued and then broke into the **debugger** with Ctl-C. Below is an example of the commands used and responses received from GDB/OpenOCD.

```
(gdb) break LedOn
Breakpoint 1 at 0x8188: file ../../boards/rpi/board.c, line 126.
(gdb) continue
Continuing.
cannot read system control register in this mode

Breakpoint 1, LedOn () at ../../boards/rpi/board.c:126
(gdb) bt
#0  LedOn () at ../../boards/rpi/board.c:126
#1  0x00008220 in microsleep (microseconds=0) at ../../boards/rpi/boar
Backtrace stopped: previous frame inner to this frame (corrupt stack?)
(gdb) delete breakpoints
Delete all breakpoints? (y or n) y
(gdb) continue
Continuing.
target rpi3.a53.0 was not halted when resume was requested
cannot read system control register in this mode
The target is not running when halt was requested, stopping GDB.

Program received signal SIGINT, Interrupt.
LedOn () at ../../boards/rpi/board.c:126
(gdb) bt
#0  LedOn () at ../../boards/rpi/board.c:126
#1  0x00008094 in main () at main.c:76
(gdb)
```

Lab 5: System Timers

5.1 Why is a timer important?

The hardware timer is the foundation on which a systems engineer can create software for more complex hardware interfaces. A software timer has many uses when developing system software. Combined with the ability to turn on the LED, a timer interface can be used to blink detailed error codes with a sequence of LED flashes. When first bringing up new hardware it is important to verify and integrate the hardware timer into a software interface. Oftentimes a system problem is the result of a timer or timing problem. A reliable timer with an easy to use interface is the foundation of quality system software.

The Raspberry Pi has a memory mapped interface to a hardware clock running at microsecond, or 1MHZ, precision. Referencing the BCM2835-ARM-Peripheral.pdf document, section 12.1, this chapters goal is to understand the Raspberry Pi timer interface (12.1 System Timer Registers). This BCM2835 document, and others like it, can be confusing because they are authored for such a wide audience. From a systems software perspective the key to deciphering these documents is to focus on the software interface, or hardware registers exposed to software. The 32 bit timer status, as well as low and high count, are the only registers required to create a complete system interface for the hardware timer.

5.2 Configure board.h for Raspberry Pi timer

The RPi hardware has a fixed memory map configuration so the offset address of the peripherals has not yet changed across hardware revisions. The timer offset address is 0x003000, relative to the peripheral base address which depends on the RPI hardware version. Add this definition to board.h, just above the GPIO_BASE defined in the previous chapter, if it is not there already. This value was discovered in the Raspberry Pi hardware documentation, BCM2835-ARM-Peripherals.pdf page 172.

Also for readability, we are changing the name RPI_BASE to PERIPHERAL_BASE and using it when assigning the address for each hardware register.

```
#define TIMER_BASE        (PERIPHERAL_BASE | 0x003000)
```

Next we must use the TIMER_BASE to define the specific timer registers we will use to create our timer functions. Let use define these at the bottom of board.h now.

```
/*
 * Timer registers
*/
#define TIMER_CS          (TIMER_BASE | 0x00) // clock status
#define TIMER_CLO         (TIMER_BASE | 0x04) // clock low 32 bytes
#define TIMER_CHI         (TIMER_BASE | 0x08) // clock high 32 bytes
```

5.3 System Software Interface to LED

Using the LED source code from the previous chapter as an example, create a system software interface for the LED. The software interface should split the functionality in the Chapter 4 main.c into three global functions, BoardInit(), LedOn() and LedOff() and it should declare the functions global in system.h. These global functions are hardware specific so the functions themselves should be created in the file 'boards/rpi/board.c'. For BoardInit() we put the level select and GPIO configure code from the previous chapter that initializes the LED. The turning on and off of the LED should go in the global LedOn() and LedOff() functions. This should be the resulting file structure:

```
Lab5 Timed LED
    applications
        errorstatus
            main.c
    boards
        rpi
            board.c
            board.h
    include
        system.h
```

While reorganizing is good for the long run, it does make the compilation process a bit more complicated as header files and source files are now in different directories. After creating the the new files and directory structure, the build script will also need to be updated.

The updated 'build.bat/build.sh' is below. Note the option '-I' adds an include file path which define the paths, relative to the application directory. It moves back two directories ('../..') to get to the 'include' or 'boards' directory since the build.bat script is executing now in the 'applications/errorstatus' directory.

```
#options -ffreestanding prevent linking in GNU stuff
#option -c compiles/assembles, -O2 optimizes

# RPI 2
# options -DRPI=2 for RPi 2
# RPI B+
#option -DRPI=1 for RPi B+

arm-none-eabi-gcc -c -DRPI=3 -ffreestanding -I. -I../../include -I../.\
./boards/rpi -o main.o main.c
arm-none-eabi-gcc -c -DRPI=3 -ffreestanding -I. -I../../include -I../.\
./boards/rpi -o ..\..\boards\rpi\board.o ..\..\boards\rpi\board.c

#Use ld to link with RPi memory map
arm-none-eabi-ld -T ../../boards/rpi/memory.map -o errorcodes.elf main\
.o ../../boards/rpi/board.o
```

```
#strip elf into binary and copy to kernel.img
arm-none-eabi-objcopy errorcodes.elf -O binary errorcodes.bin
cp errorcodes.bin kernel.img
```

Here are the generic board global function declarations to add to system.h.

```
/*
 * Board interface
*/
void BoardInit(void);
void LedOn(void);
void LedOff(void);
```

Add/move the code in main.c from past chapter to the new function BoardInit() within board.c. Create the file and BoardInit() function now if you have not already done so. Afterward, add the LedOn() and LedOff() functions below to the end of the board.c file.

```
/*...................................................................*/
/*      LedOn: Turn on the activity LED                              */
/*                                                                   */
/*...................................................................*/
void LedOn(void)
{
  /* Turn on the activity LED. */
#if RPI == 4
  /* RPI 4 has LED at GPIO 42, so set GPIO 42. */
  REG32(GPSET1) = 1 << (42 - 32);
#elif RPI == 3
  /* RPI 3 has LED at GPIO 29, so set GPIO 29. */
  REG32(GPSET0) = 1 << 29;
#else
  /* Other RPIs have LED at GPIO 47, so set GPIO 47. */
  REG32(GPSET1) = 1 << (47 - 32);
#endif
```

```
}

/*.....................................................................*/
/*      LedOff: Turn off the activity LED                              */
/*                                                                     */
/*.....................................................................*/
void LedOff(void)
{
  /* Turn off the activity LED. */
#if RPI == 4
  /* RPI 4 has LED at GPIO 42, so clear GPIO 42. */
  REG32(GPCLR1) = 1 << (42 - 32);
#elif RPI == 3
  /* RPI 3 has LED at GPIO 29, so clear GPIO 29. */
  REG32(GPCLR0) = 1 << 29;
#else
  /* Other RPIs have LED at GPIO 47, so clear GPIO 47. */
  REG32(GPCLR1) = 1 << (47 - 32);
#endif
}
```

Combine this change with the timer and sleep functions created in the main book to create an application that loops forever, alternating between turning the LED on for one second and off for one second. The timer functions created in the book require one modification, the TIMER_CLOCK defined is generic and must be changed to be RPi specific. Please change the code to use the RPI low timer register name TIMER_CLO instead of TIMER_CLOCK. Then create a new main.c as below that should blink the LED activity light upon execution.

```
/*
 * Loop, turning the led on and off.
*/
for (;;)
{
  LedOn();
  Sleep(1);
  LedOff();
  Sleep(1);
}
```

5.4 New application "errorcodes"

System software now exists to turn the LED on or off as well as to keep time. Using these functions, create an algorithm to turn the single LED on and off in a sequence that can represent a one byte value (0 - 255). The function should repeat the sequence repeatedly in a manner so that the observer will know when the sequence begins.

One way to do this is repeat the sequence of the error number. A long delay between repeats and a shorter delay between digits could allow a user to count two consecutive nibble values, allowing an entire byte to be communicated as an informative error code.

There are many ways to create this solution. The answer below splits the error code into two hexadecimal digits, or nibbles, and flashes the two numbers in the range of 0 through 15, one after the other with a short pause between. After both numbers are blinked, there is a longer pause before the sequence is repeated. Please review the code and comments now.

main.c

```
/*..............................................................*/
/*        main: Application Entry Point                         */
/*                                                              */
/*     Returns: Exit error                                      */
/*..............................................................*/
int main(void)
{
  u8 i, code, tmp;

  /* Initialize the hardware. */
  BoardInit();

  /* Loop, testing different error codes in increments of one. */
  for (code = 1;; ++code)
  {
    /* Shift high order nibble of code into tmp and clear rest. */
    tmp = ((code >> 4) & 0xF);

    /* Loop, blinking LED the number of times of the nibble value. */
    for (i = 0; i < tmp; ++i)
    {
      LedOn();
      usleep(MICROS_PER_SECOND / 4); /* quarter second on */
      LedOff();
      usleep(MICROS_PER_SECOND / 4); /* quarter second off */
    }

    /* Wait one second to indicate to user the next nibble. */
    Sleep(1);

    /* Put low order nibble of code into tmp. */
    tmp = code & 0xF;

    /* Loop, blinking LED the number of times of the nibble value. */
    for (i = 0; i < tmp; ++i)
    {
```

```
        LedOn();
        usleep(MICROS_PER_SECOND / 4); /* quarter second on */
        LedOff();
        usleep(MICROS_PER_SECOND / 4); /* quarter second off */
      }

      /* Wait three seconds to indicate to user the next byte. */
      Sleep(3);
    }
    return 0;
}
```

Most of the code is straight forward and described clearly in the comments, however let us review the creation of the low and high order nibbles. The code 'code & 0xF' ANDs the error code variable 'code' with a nibble of all ones (0xF), causing the high order nibble to be removed from the byte and only the low order nibble to remain. The code '((code >> 4) & 0xF)' uses the right shift operator '>>' to shift the high order 4 bit nibble to the right 4 bits and into the low order position. It then does the same '& 0xF' to ensure only the low order nibble remains.

5.5 Using Make to create an executable binary

Make can greatly simplify and add reliability to the compiling and linking process. As the number of files to compile grows the more complicated the build.sh script becomes. The first step to using Make is to ensure it is installed on the development PC and install it if not. Open a system shell (Terminal or Command Prompt) and try the command 'make'. If the command is not found, Make must be installed. On Linux this can usually be performed with this command:

```
$ sudo apt-get install make
```

Windows users are encouraged to use the PowerShell, or install MinGW and MSYS which provides a system shell with many extra Unix commands including make (see chapter 2 lab). Please take the time now to install 'Make' and check that it is usable. With 'Make' installed, let us create a new file named 'Makefile' and copy the example

'Makefile' from the main book, section 5.4, into this file. Two options need to be added to the 'Makefile' for GCC to build correctly for the specific RPi hardware, the EXTRAS and ASFLAGS definitions. Also, the changes are different depending on whether the hardware is an RPi B+, 2 or 3. First let us review the RPi B+ changes, adding -DRPI=1 to the EXTRAS definition. These options were discussed in chapter 3 and used in the build shell script. Now we need to be sure to add them to the Makefile and enable the specific options for the RPi hardware we are creating software for.

```
EXTRAS = -DRPI=3 -ffreestanding
ASFLAGS =
```

Next let us review the RPi 2 changes needed to the base Makefile to reflect the difference in CPUs.

```
EXTRAS = -DRPI=2 -ffreestanding
ASFLAGS =
```

Now that Make is installed and the Makefile is configured for the RPi, let us review the new simplified process to create system software that is executable on bare metal. Here a single make command is used to compile and link the entire bare metal application. While not a huge time saver now, this will become increasingly helpful as the number of files grow. It is also very helpful to have the 'make clean' command available, to clean out the old compiled binaries so we can perform a fresh build. Alternatively to the procedure below, the software creator may use GDB and JTAG/OpenOCD to 'load' the newly created application and 'continue' to execute it, instead of copying to the SD card.

```
$ make
arm-none-eabi-gcc -c -Wall -O2 -DRPI=3 -ffreestanding -I. -o main.o ma\
in.c
arm-none-eabi-ld -T memory.map -o app.elf main.o
arm-none-eabi-objcopy app.elf -O binary app.bin
cp app.bin kernel7.img

$
[MOVE SD TO PC, E: DRIVE]
```

```
$ cp app.bin e:\kernel7.img
[DISCONNECT SD/USB IN OS]
[MOVE SD BACK TO RPI]
[POWER ON]
<* Program runs *>
```

Make checks time stamps of the source files so if a source code file (.c) has been modified more recently then the associated output file (.o), Make will compile this file. However, Make does not by default check for header file changes, so if a common header file changes it is very important to recompile all source code files. The easy way to do this is with the “make clean” command. Let us review the last example for this laboratory assignment that cleans the application and compiles it again from scratch.

It is not at all required to understand the entirety of the Makefile syntax. However, the INCLUDES definition is very important since it contains a list of file system paths that are to be searched, in order, for header files needed during the compilation process. Any header file in any of these directories will be available to a .c file during compilation, for example ‘#include <board.h>’. Otherwise a full path (absolute or relative to the application) path enclosed in quotes is needed when including header files ‘#include “../../include/board.h”’ within a .c file.

Another very important definition is the OBJECTS definition which includes all the source objects that should be compiled to create the resulting executable. In this example we have created a new board.c file so it needs to be added to the Makefile. Since the first code to be executed is the first to be linked, main.c should be the first object in the OBJECTS list. This will be explained and expanded upon in more detail in the following chapters.

```
$ make clean
rm -f main.o
rm -f *.bin
rm -f *.elf
rm -f *.img
```

```
$ make
arm-none-eabi-gcc -c -Wall -O2 -DRPI=3 -ffreestanding -I. -I../../incl\
ude -I../../boards/rpi -o main.o main.c
arm-none-eabi-gcc -c -Wall -O2 -DRPI=3 -ffreestanding -I. -I../../incl\
```

```
ude -I../../boards/rpi -o ../../boards/rpi/board.o ../../boards/rpi/bo\
ard.c
arm-none-eabi-ld -T memory.map -o errorcodes.elf ../../boards/rpi/boar\
d.o main.o
arm-none-eabi-objcopy errorcodes.elf -O binary errorcodes.bin
cp errorcodes.bin kernel7.img
$
```

Let us review the completed Makefile now. Note that this Makefile includes RPi revision optimization flags for building and the EXTRAS and ASFLAGS lines need to be commented out and the existing commented lines used instead for the RPi 2/3.

```
#
# Makefile for errorcodes application
#

##
## Commands:
##
CP   = cp
RM   = rm
C = arm-none-eabi-gcc
CC   = arm-none-eabi-gcc
LINK   = arm-none-eabi-ld
PLINK= arm-none-eabi-objcopy

##
## Definitions:
##
APPNAME = app

# Define the RPI hardware version: 1 through 4
EXTRAS = -DRPI=3 -ffreestanding
ASFLAGS =

##Warnings about everything and optimize for size or speed (-Os or -O2)
```

```
#CFLAGS = -Wall -O2 $(EXTRAS)

##Warnings and debugging build, with GDB and no optimizations (-O0)
CFLAGS = -Wall -ggdb -O0 $(EXTRAS)
INCLUDES = -I. -I../../include -I../../boards/rpi

##
## Application
##
OBJECTS = main.o \
          ../../boards/rpi/board.o \

##
## Define build commands for the C and assembly source file types
##
.c.o:
  $(CC) -c $(CFLAGS) $(INCLUDES) -o $@ $<

.s.o:
  $(AS) $(ASFLAGS) -o $@ $<

##
## Targets
##
all:  object

object: $(OBJECTS)
  $(LINK) -T ../../boards/rpi/memory.map -o $(APPNAME).elf $(OBJECTS)
  $(PLINK) $(APPNAME).elf -O binary $(APPNAME).bin
  $(CP) $(APPNAME).bin kernel7.img

clean:
  rm -f $(OBJECTS)
  rm -f *.bin
  rm -f *.elf
  rm -f *.img
```

5.6 Complete 64 bit timer for RPi

In the companion book we introduced an algorithm that had software maintain the roll over of a single 32 bit time register. While that was a good exercise and is required on some hardware, the RPi includes two hardware registers, one for the low order 32 bits of the timer, and other for the high order 32 bits of the counter. Because of this there is no need for software to maintain the roll over. Let us upgrade our timer routines to use both low and high order timer registers and thus simplify the algorithm.

First let us be sure not to change the public interface so that usleep() remains the same, and the parameters and return values of TimerRegister() and TimeRemaining() are the same. Let us review the changes to TimerRegister and TimerRemaining() now.

```
/*...................................................................*/
/* TimerRegister: Register an expiration time                        */
/*                                                                   */
/*       Input: microseconds until timer expires                     */
/*                                                                   */
/*     Returns: resulting expiration time                            */
/*...................................................................*/
struct timer TimerRegister(u64 microseconds)
{
  struct timer tw;
  u64 now;

  /* Retrieve the current time from the 1MHZ hardware clock. */
  now = REG32(TIMER_CLO);  /* low order time */
  now |= ((u64)REG32(TIMER_CHI) << 32); /* high order time */

  /* Calculate and return the expiration time of the new timer. */
  tw.expire = now + microseconds;

  /* Return the created timer. */
  return tw;
}
```

```
/*..............................................................*/
/* TimerRemaining: Check if a registered timer has expired      */
/*                                                              */
/*      Input: expire - clock time of expiration in microseconds */
/*             unused - unused on RPi as it has 64 bit precision */
/*                                                              */
/*    Returns: Zero (0) or microseconds until timer expiration  */
/*..............................................................*/
u64 TimerRemaining(struct timer *tw)
{
  u64 now;

  /* Retrieve the current time from the 1MHZ hardware clock. */
  now = REG32(TIMER_CLO); /* low order time */
  now |= ((u64)REG32(TIMER_CHI) << 32); /* high order time */

  /* Return zero if timer expired. */
  if (now > tw->expire)
    return 0;

  /* Return time until expiration if not expired. */
  return tw->expire - now;
}

/*..............................................................*/
/*   TimerNow: Return the current time in clock ticks           */
/*                                                              */
/*..............................................................*/
u64 TimerNow(void)
{
  u64 now;

  /* Retrieve the current time from the 1MHZ hardware clock. */
  now = REG32(TIMER_CLO); /* low order time */
  now |= ((u64)REG32(TIMER_CHI) << 32); /* high order time */
```

```
/*
** Return the current time.
*/
return now;
:
```

Lab 6: UART Peripheral

6.1 Why the UART?

The UART peripheral is a simple and versatile hardware peripheral available on the RPi and the next step to creating functional system software. A UART can send data at moderate speeds in either direction between the development PC and the RPi executing our software creations. A UART is commonly used for a terminal or command shell, so that the development PC can issue commands to execute on the other system and receive responses. It is the creation of this shell interface that is the goal of this chapter, as connecting the development PC to an RPi running a UART command shell allows many execution and diagnostic options to speed up future software development efforts. For example, error strings can be sent over the UART to be displayed on the development PC in order to speed up the discovery and resolution of future problems.

An easily expandable command line shell interface executing on the Raspberry Pi is a great tool to aid system software development. With the physical UART connection, the development PC can enter a shell environment and execute any commands the application has made available. Command results, along with logging and error messages are also possible. Let the journey be as interesting as the destination.

6.2 Raspberry Pi UART Register Address Map

Chapter 6 of the companion book created a generic UART system software interface designed for the common 16C650 compatible UART hardware interface. The Raspberry Pi primary UART is a PL011 UART which is partially 16C650 compatible. With some additional configuration, the UART interface created in the main book should be ready to run and test on the RPi. First, reference the BCM2835-ARM-Peripherals.pdf, Chapter 13 UART. In section 13.4 is the UART Address Map.

The first coding step is to add the UART base definition to board.h, after the TIMER_-BASE definition.

```
#define UART0_BASE       (PERIPHERAL_BASE | 0x201000)
```

The next goal is to review the UART Address Map and define names and address locations for the hardware registers in the memory map to represent software pointers, for example '#define UART0_DATA (UART0_BASE + 0x00)'. Please add UART0_ to each register name so it is recognized as a memory mapped register of the UART. For clarity, please rename RSRECR register defined in the BCM2835 document to UART0_RX_STATUS, FR to UART0_STATUS, LCRH to UART0_LINE_CTRL and CR to UART0_CONTROL. This makes the registers easier to read and understand, as well as portable to other hardware systems that do not use the BCM2835 syntax for register naming. These are also the names used in the main book so the code can be used with minimal changes. Let us review these defined register addresses now.

```
/*
 * UART (16C650) register map
*/
#define UART0_DATA        (UART0_BASE + 0x00)
#define UART0_RX_STATUS   (UART0_BASE + 0x04)
#define UART0_STATUS      (UART0_BASE + 0x18)
#define UART0_ILPR        (UART0_BASE + 0x20)
#define UART0_IBRD        (UART0_BASE + 0x24)
#define UART0_FBRD        (UART0_BASE + 0x28)
#define UART0_LINE_CTRL   (UART0_BASE + 0x2C)
#define UART0_CONTROL     (UART0_BASE + 0x30)
#define UART0_IFLS        (UART0_BASE + 0x34)
#define UART0_IMSC        (UART0_BASE + 0x38)
#define UART0_RIS         (UART0_BASE + 0x3C)
#define UART0_MIS         (UART0_BASE + 0x40)
#define UART0_ICR         (UART0_BASE + 0x44)
#define UART0_DMACR       (UART0_BASE + 0x48)
#define UART0_ITCR        (UART0_BASE + 0x80)
#define UART0_ITIP        (UART0_BASE + 0x84)
#define UART0_ITOP        (UART0_BASE + 0x88)
#define UART0_TDR         (UART0_BASE + 0x8C)
```

6.3 Raspberry Pi UART Register Details

The goal of this section is to analyze the registers and create sub definitions for each of the configuration and status bits that the system software needs to access. First let use review the register details for UART0_DATA (page 179 of BCM2835-ARM-Peripherals.pdf) and create these definitions for the 32 bit data register. The first 8 bytes are the data followed by error bits. The final definition combines all errors into a single definition DATA_ERROR so all errors can be checked at once. RX_DATA can be used with the 'And' (&) operation in C to extract the 8 bits of data from the 32 bit UART0_DATA register, for example 'data = REG32(UART_DATA) & RX_DATA'.

```
#define UART0_DATA        (UART0_BASE + 0x00)
#define   RX_DATA                 (0xFF << 0)
#define   DR_FRAME_ERROR          (1 << 8)
#define   DR_PARITY_ERROR         (1 << 9)
#define   DR_BREAK_ERROR          (1 << 10)
#define   DR_OVERRUN_ERROR        (1 << 11)
#define     DATA_ERROR    (DR_FRAME_ERROR | DR_PARITY_ERROR | \
                           DR_BREAK_ERROR | DR_OVERRUN_ERROR)
```

Next we do the same with UART0_RX_STATUS (page 180 of BCM2835-ARM-Peripherals.pdf). The UART0_RX_STATUS defines four different errors and an RX_-ERROR define that is a combination of all four errors, similar to the DATA_ERROR definition above.

```
#define UART0_RX_STATUS  (UART0_BASE + 0x04)
#define   RX_FRAME_ERROR          (1 << 0)
#define   RX_PARITY_ERROR         (1 << 1)
#define   RX_BREAK_ERROR          (1 << 2)
#define   RX_OVERRUN_ERROR        (1 << 3)
#define     RX_ERROR      (RX_FRAME_ERROR | RX_PARITY_ERROR | \
                           RX_BREAK_ERROR | RX_OVERRUN_ERROR)
```

Next move on to the UART0_STATUS (page 181 of BCM2835-ARM-Peripherals.pdf). The UART status register contains important information, such as whether the UART Rx FIFO buffer is empty, which means there is no data available to read. Also, to avoid

Tx errors it is important for the system software to wait before sending data if the Tx FIFO is full. The UART status is the dashboard for the UART controller. The use of these UART registers is an important step in understanding most other hardware to software interfaces.

```
#define UART0_STATUS      (UART0_BASE + 0x18)
#define   CLEAR_TO_SEND          (1 << 0)
#define   BUSY                   (1 << 3)
#define   RX_FIFO_EMPTY          (1 << 4)
#define   TX_FIFO_FULL           (1 << 5)
#define   RX_FIFO_FULL           (1 << 6)
#define   TX_FIFO_EMPTY          (1 << 7)
```

Next is the UART0_LINE_CTRL (page 184 of BCM2835-ARM-Peripherals.pdf) register. The UART line control register contains the configuration options for the UART serial channel. It can be used to set the word size, parity and stop bits. While it is highly encouraged to leave size, parity and stop bits at the default configuration, the ENABLE_FIFO bit will turn on Rx and Tx FIFO queues that increase speed and reliability of the UART hardware interface. A hardware FIFO queue allows system software to send multiple bytes at a time (Tx FIFO) and for hardware to receive multiple bytes (Rx FIFO) before requiring service by software. Turning on ENABLE_FIFO should increase speed and/ reduce data corruption errors at high speeds.

```
#define UART0_LINE_CTRL   (UART0_BASE + 0x2C)
#define   BREAK                  (1 << 0)
#define   PARITY                 (1 << 1)
#define   EVEN_PARITY            (1 << 2)
#define   TWO_STOP_BITS          (1 << 3)
#define   ENABLE_FIFO            (1 << 4)
#define   BYTE_WORD_LENGTH       (3 << 5)
#define   STICK_PARITY           (1 << 7)
```

Last is the UART0_CONTROL (page 185 of BCM2835-ARM-Peripherals.pdf) register. The UART control register contains the configuration options for the UART hardware controller. Included are an Rx and Tx enable as well as an overall Enable bit. If the

UART requires reconfiguring, the UART enable bit should be cleared (set to zero) to disable the UART. It is good design to check and wait until the UART0_STATUS is not Busy before disabling or outgoing data may be lost/corrupted. Once disabled, the UART can be reconfigured and then restarted by setting the UART enable bit to one (1). RTS and CTS are hardware flow control options that require additional GPIO wires on the physical UART connection. Hardware flow control can add reliability to the data transfers but may not eliminate all loss or transfer errors. Let us define these bits now for completeness and to aid this future effort.

```
#define UART0_CONTROL      (UART0_BASE + 0x30)
#define   ENABLE                   (1 << 0)
#define   LOOPBACK                 (1 << 7)
#define   TX_ENABLE                (1 << 8)
#define   RX_ENABLE                (1 << 9)
#define   RTS                      (1 << 11)
#define   RTS_FLOW_CONTROL         (1 << 14)
#define   CTS_FLOW_CONTROL         (1 << 15)
```

6.4 GPIO configuration for RPi UART

The interface to the primary UART on the Raspberry Pi is through the GPIO header pins on the motherboard. These pins need to be configured for the UART, which means setting the GPIO function select alternate number and disabling the pull up or pull down resistors for the UART Rx and Tx GPIOs. The pull up/down GPIO resistors must be disabled so that the UART hardware controller can take control of the GPIO pins without the interference of a resistor. With a pull up or pull down resistor in place the UART controller will have difficulty driving the Rx and Tx data transfers. Add this code to UartInit() created in Chapter 6.3 of the book, in between disabling the UART and configuring the baud rate divisor and enabling. Replace example baud rate divisor code with the RPI specific code below.

```
  /* Select Alternate 0 for UART over GPIO pins 14 Tx and 15 Rx.*/
  gpio = REG32(GPFSEL1);
  gpio &= ~(7 << 12); /* clear GPIO 14 */
  gpio |= GPIO_ALT0 << 12; /* set GPIO 14 to Alt 0 */
  gpio &= ~(7 << 15); /* clear GPIO 15 */
  gpio |= GPIO_ALT0 << 15; /* set GPIO 15 to Alt 0 */
  REG32(GPFSEL1) = gpio;

  /*
  ** GPPUD can be 0 (disable pull up/down)
  ** (0) disable pull up and pull down to float the GPIO
  ** (1 << 0) enable pull down (low)
  ** (1 << 1) enable pull up (high)
  */

  /* Disable pull up/down for next configured GPIOs so they float. */
  REG32(GPPUD) = GPPUD_OFF;
  usleep(MICROS_PER_MILLISECOND); /* hold time */

  /* Apply above configuration (floating) to UART Rx and Tx GPIOs. */
  REG32(GPPUDCLK0) = (1 << 14) | (1 << 15); /* GPIO 14 and 15 */
  usleep(MICROS_PER_MILLISECOND); /* hold time */

  /* Set the baud rate. */
#if RPI >= 3
  // RPI 3/4 has a 48MHz clock as it was intended to work with BT
  //(48000000 / (16 * 115200) = 26.042
  //(0.042*64)+0.5 = 3
  //115200 baud is int 26 frac 3
  REG32(UART0_IBRD) = 26; /* Integer baud rate divisor */
  REG32(UART0_FBRD) = 3; /* Fractional baud rate divisor */
#else
  // RPI 1/2 has a 3MHz clock by default
  //(3000000 / (16 * 115200) = 1.627
  //(0.627*64)+0.5 = 40
  //115200 baud is int 1 frac 40
```

```
  REG32(UART0_IBRD) = 1; /* Integer baud rate divisor */
  REG32(UART0_FBRD) = 40; /* Fractional baud rate divisor */
#endif
```

Notice there are often usleep calls, or a hold time, to the GPIO configuration procedure. This hold time is used to ensure that the previous register assignment has completed and the peripheral is ready for the next assignment. Without the working timer and sleep software interface we created in chapter 5, it would not be possible to consistently initialize and configure the UART. This hold time requirement is defined on page 101 of the BCM2835 document.

The default UART clock on the RPi 1 and 2 is 3MHz, the same as the example in the companion book. In fact, RPi UART can use the code in the companion book directly, except for the RPi 3 and 4 which have a faster clock. The baud divisor must be configured so as to drive the UART data transfer at the correct baud rate. With the RPi 1 and 2 it is always recommended to double check the boot settings of the UART. In the boot file system of the RPi being used for testing (the one we copy the kernel.img to), check that in the /boot/config.txt file that the 'init_uart_clock=3000000' option is set (not commented out). If a different UART clock rate is configured only garbage will appear over the UART when connecting with the development PC, as the clock divisor depends on the shared system clock connected to it.

6.5 Command line application

The next step is to create a new application named 'console' that can be used to send commands and receive responses. In the applications directory create a directory named 'console' and copy all the files from the previous chapters application, 'errorcodes', to the new directory. Open Makefile and change APPNAME from 'errorcodes' to 'console' and add '../../boards/rpi/uart0.o' and '../../system/shell.o' to the OBJECTS declaration.

```
##
## Error code application
##
OBJECTS = ../../boards/rpi/boot.o \
          ../../boards/rpi/board.o \
          ../../boards/rpi/uart0.o \
          ../../system/shell.o \
          main.o \
```

Now create the file 'boards/rpi/uart0.c' and copy all the UART functions from Chapter 6 to this file (UartInit(), UartPutc(), UartPuts(), UartRxCheck() and UartGetc()). Next copy the additional RPi specific UART configuration code above (level select and disabling of GPIO pull up/down) to the middle of the UartInit() function. Finally, create the 'system/shell.c' file copy the system shell code from the end of Chapter 6 to this file. The goal of this section is to put together all of the source code and create a 'console' application that presents a command line shell interface over the UART peripheral. Combined with the Makefile changes above, the 'console' application should now compile without errors or warnings.

6.6 USB to serial TTL connection

So the system software now has UART support, but how can the development PC use this? The first requirement is to have the appropriate hardware connection. There are many options for using the UART but this book will discuss two. The first option is the simplest, the Raspberry Pi has a 3.3 volt TTL interface to the UART through the GPIO pins. If you have two Raspberry Pi systems then the UART GPIO pins can be connected directly with female to female jumper wires. The second option is for those with only one Raspberry Pi or those who want to use a different PC for the software development. For full Linux or Windows development systems (desktop, laptop, etc.) there is typically no TTL UART available on GPIO pins and if there is it may not be accessible or documented for the motherboard. So it is recommended to use a USB to serial TTL adapter to connect the Raspberry Pi to the development PC, whether using a Linux OS or Windows OS.

Warning

The RPi UART GPIO pins are 3.3V TTL and if connected directly to a standard serial (DB9) cable typical of legacy PC systems it will destroy the Raspberry Pi. This is because the serial DB9 connection uses 5 volts and this voltage is too high.

Before we discuss the specific instructions for each method of connecting the UART, let us discuss some commonalities. First, the UART serial communication model is serial cross over in that the Rx from one side of the connection must be connected to the Tx side on the other end. So when the RPi sends, the development PC is receiving. And vice versa the other way so when the development PC sends, the RPi is receiving. This configuration is commonly referred to as a crossover connection. With this in mind, see Section 6.2 (page 102) of the BCM2835-ARM-Peripherals.pdf document for the complete GPIO map for the Raspberry Pi, including all the alternate functions. The primary UART interface is highlighted in red and named RXD0 and TXD0 and available on select alternate zero (Alt 0). Note that TXD0 is GPIO 14, and RXD0 is GPIO 15 and located at pin 8 and 10 respectively on the exposed male pins of the RPi. Here is a picture created by Jamie Bainbridge that shows all the GPIOs of the RPi as exposed by the male pins.

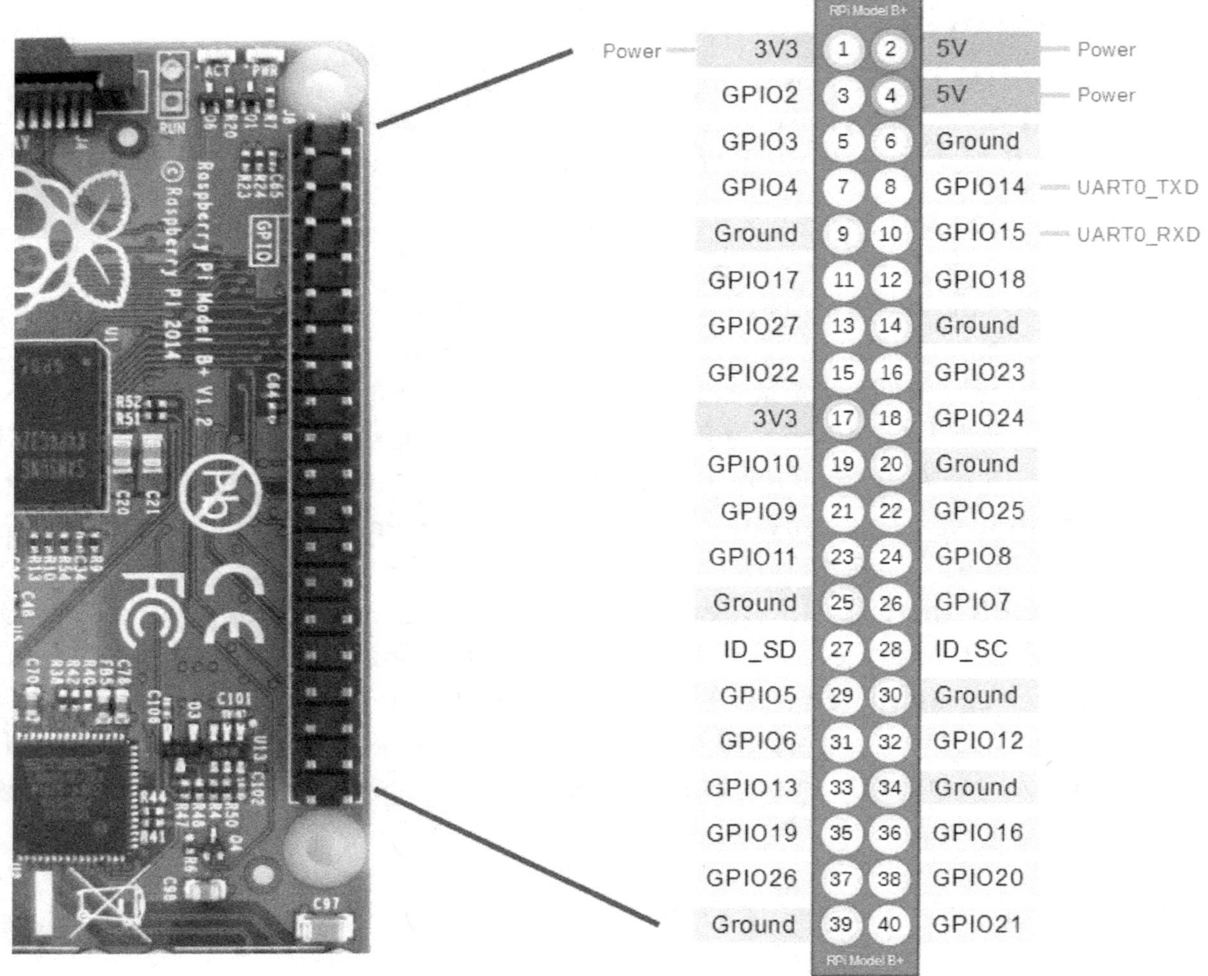

Fig 6: Raspberry Pi GPIO pinout

6.6.1 Connect UART between two RPi's

Wiring the TTL UART between two different Raspberry Pi's is relatively straightforward. First, power off both boards just to be safe (if you bump live wires together, etc. it could damage one or both RPi's). Second, using a female to female jumper wire, connect the ground (GND) nearest the UART GPIO pins (this would be the Ground (GND) at pin 6) with a gray or black wire. It is always good practice to use gray or black for GND and red or yellow for power (PWR) and the other colors for everything else. It is also good practice to always connect the ground (GND) of the peripheral to the ground nearest the GPIO connectors the peripheral is going to use. Grounding nearby GPIO pins avoids static build up between the systems and may reduce errors during data transfers.

Fig 7: UART pin map for RPI development PC to RPI target

GPIO	Pin	Pin	GPIO	UART line
15	8	10	14	TX to RX
14	10	8	15	RX to TX
-	6	6	-	Ground

Once the USB to TTL UART is grounded to the RPi, connect the UART0 TX (pin 8) of the first RPi to the UART0 RX (pin 10) of the second RPi. Do the same for the UART0 RX (pin 10) of the first RPi, connecting it to the UART0 TX (pin 8) of the second RPi. Now boot up the development RPi and the UART should be operational as the device '/dev/serial0' or '/dev/ttyAMA0'.

Information

Recent versions of RPI hardware often disable the primary UART. To ensure the RPI boots with primary UART edit the /boot/config.txt of the RPI executing the UART code and add enable_uart=1 to the end of the file. Reboot the development RPI with this change and see if it not works.

6.6.2 UART software for Linux development PC

Linux users should check to ensure they have 'minicom' installed on the development RPi and if not, issue the command 'sudo apt-get install minicom' to install it. With 'minicom' installed let us connect the two RPi UART's physically as described in section 6.6.1, or with a USB to TTL UART as described in section 6.6.3 below if you have not done so yet. Then copy the 'console' binary file named 'kernel.img' onto the microSD card of the RPi that will execute it (or use GDB to 'load' it). Then open 'minicom' on the '/dev/serial0' device on the Linux development PC with this command.

```
$ sudo minicom -D /dev/serial0

Welcome to minicom 2.7

OPTIONS: I18n
Compiled on Feb  7 2016, 14:00:34.
Port /dev/serial0, 12:32:56

Press CTRL-A Z for help on special keys
```

After connecting physically and starting minicom, power on the RPi (or invoke 'continue' from GDB) to execute the software we created. The interactive shell should output its introduction splash through minicom to the development PC.

```
$ sudo minicom -D /dev/serial0

Welcome to minicom 2.7

OPTIONS: I18n
Compiled on Feb  7 2016, 14:00:34.
Port /dev/serial0, 12:32:56

Press CTRL-A Z for help on special keys

Console application running on Raspberry Pi
  Copyright 2015 Sean Lawless, All rights reserved.

Check timer. Sleep 1s loop. Press key to exit.
1234

Check timer. Sleep 1/10s loop. Press key to exit.
12345678901234567890123456

Entering the system shell
shell>
```

If you connected after powering on it is no big deal, but you will miss the introductory splash so you will probably witness the numbers counting by in second increments until you press a key. If you see garbage characters, the baud rate divisor and/or UART clock are not configured correctly.

Important

Often the Linux OS installed on the RPi development PC (Raspbian, etc.) will by default configure and use the primary UART for a Linux shell console. This means that the RPi development PC's serial device '/dev/serial0' will be in use as a Linux command shell after boot up. This will interfere with the development RPi when we connect to it. To avoid this interference, be sure to disable the Linux console on the serial0 device at boot up on the development. For Raspbian on the RPi, remove the 'console=...' line from the /boot/cmdline.txt file so Linux will not use the UART as a command line console. Reboot the development RPI with this change and the UART should works better.

The last step is to add privileges to the Linux OS user to use 'minicom' so that the 'sudo' command is not needed. 'Sudo' elevates the user privilege to the superuser which is not a good security practice. The serial devices, such as '/dev/serial0', are only accessible to the superuser as well as the user group 'dialout'. To avoid using 'sudo' with the '/dev/serial0' device, add the 'dialout' group to your user group settings. This can be done with this command, replacing <username> with the name of your user.

```
$ sudo usermod -a -G dialout <username>
```

Then log out from your user account (or reboot) and upon the next log in the user will be able to use 'minicom' with the '/dev/serial0' device without superuser privilege.

```
$ minicom -D /dev/serial0

Welcome to minicom 2.7

OPTIONS: I18n
Compiled on Feb  7 2016, 14:00:34.
Port /dev/serial0, 12:32:56

Press CTRL-A Z for help on special keys
```

6.6.3 Connect UART from RPi to PC

Using a Windows or Linux system for development requires additional hardware, specifically a USB to TTL serial cable to connect between the development PC and the Raspberry Pi. The easiest to use solution has a USB connection on one end, and two to five female jumper wires on the other end. The jumper wires connect to the Raspberry Pi GPIOs directly exposed on the RPi board as male pins. Only two are really needed, Rx and Tx, but the ground should also be connected if available. As of this writing, there are USB to UART TTL's for under $10 USD online. Make sure it is for TTL (3.3 volts) and the USB device is compatible with the development PC's Operating System. It also should have individual wires on the non-USB end to connect to the RPi, preferably female connectors.

Important

Remember this is a cross over connection, so connect the Tx wire coming from the USB adapter to the RX pin on the RPi, and the RX of the USB adapter to the RPi's TX pin.

Advanced users, or users who plan to be moving beyond this book, may wish to consider a more advanced USB to serial adapter, such as the FTDI FT2232. This part has a micro USB port for the development PC and two 3.3 volt TTL serial ports with male connectors. With some female to female jumper wires, and careful reading of the FT2232 data sheet, the FT2232 can be connected to Raspberry Pi as described above. Like the dedicated cable, the FT2232 can use three wires to connect; ground, Rx and

Tx. Be sure to cross over the RX and TX when connecting to the RPi pins and connect at least one ground on the FT2232 (nearest the UART being used) with the RPi ground nearest the UART pins (pin 6). The ground is NOT optional when using the FT2232.

With Linux OS as the development environment refer to section 6.5.2 for instructions on how to connect to the serial TTL UART with 'minicom'. For USB adapters, the serial TTL device of the USB adapter will appear in Linux under the '/dev' folder after connecting. It is not possible to know ahead of time which device (/dev) will be created/used for the USB adapter. However '/dev/ttyUSB0' is common. If '/dev/ttyUSB0' is not present or does not work, unplug the USB adapter and list the /dev directory ('ls /dev') before and after connecting the USB cable to the Linux development PC. Any new '/dev/tty*' device is the one to use. On older Linux OS's the '/dev/ttyS0' may be used by the OS.

The FT2232 also supports JTAG and can be used instead of using an RPi development PC running Raspbian and OpenOCD JTAG bit bang controller as discussed in Chapter 4. If you are not using an RPi development PC, it is recommended to connect both the RPi target UART and JTAG to the FT2232 to enable both the UART and JTAG debugging with the development PC.

6.6.4 UART Software for Windows development PC

This section explores how to install and use an application running on the development PC to connect to the Raspberry Pi over the serial UART on a Windows development PC. First the reader should search for and download serial terminal software, such as TeraTerm (or ExtraPuTTY) from the Internet.

With the USB to TTL adapter (FT2232 or otherwise) connected, run TeraTerm or ExtraPuTTY and from the Setup menu select Serial Port. In the Port field use the down arrow key to show all serial COM ports. If you have more than one and do not know which one is the Raspberry Pi, open the Windows Control Panel, then Hardware and Sound and click on Device Manager. Open Ports (COM & LPT) to see the connected Serial Ports. If you still do not know, try disconnecting the USB adapter and seeing which COM port(s) goes away in the device manager. Then configure TeraTerm or ExtraPuTTY for the Port and Baud rate of 115200. Leave the Data, Parity, Stop and Flow control settings to 8 bit, none, 1 bit (8N1) respectfully. Select Ok to connect with the Raspberry Pi.

If the 'console' application was already running before the development PC connected, then the Raspberry Pi has already sent the introductory splash and command prompt. Pressing the enter button will send the empty command and if connected to the Raspberry Pi running the 'console' application, it will receive back further characters or the command prompt '>'. The goal of this laboratory assignment is to establish the terminal shell connection with the Raspberry Pi. Congratulations if this is working. If it is not yet working, see the troubleshooting in the next section.

6.7 UART Troubleshooting

Like JTAG, there is a lot that can go wrong with the UART, from the physical connection to the software configuration on both the system software and development PC. The usual checklist is to double check the wiring and software configurations. Pay particular attention to the development PC and be sure you are connecting to the correct device (/dev/ttyX or Windows COM port), and with the correct settings, 112500 baud at 8N1. It helps to use a development system whose UART is known to work with other boards so you can limit any investigation to a single side. Below are some common problems and steps to take to solve them.

If nothing appears over the UART during the start of the 'console' applications, and repeated key presses also show nothing, there is a hardware misconfiguration. Either the TTL is not physically connected correctly, or the development PC terminal software (minicom, TeraTerm, etc.) is not using the correct physical device. There could also be a serious issue with the compiled image, such as it was compiled for a different RPI, such that board.h is pointing the PERIPHERAL_BASE to the RPi 2 even though you are executing on the RPi B+.

If garbage appears when the 'console' application begins, we know the correct device is being used by the development PC. Try pressing keys and see if more garbage appears. Double check the software configuration on both sides and be sure both are configured for 112500 baud and 8N1. Double check the '/boot/config.txt' file of the RPi executing the 'console' application and be sure the 'init_uart_clock=3000000' is not commented out or set to a different value than 3MHZ.

Lab 7: Boot Loader

7.1 Why use a boot loader on Raspberry Pi?

It is simple to explain the procedure to move the microSD card to the Pi. Attach the microSD to the development PC using a USB to SD card adapter and copy the executable kernel.img file and move the microSD back to execute on the RPi. It is also possible to use JTAG and GDB, with the 'load' command, to transfer our executables to the remote RPi for execution. So why do we need a boot loader? The reason for a boot loader when developing system software on the RPi is to have a solution outside of JTAG or the SD card dance. Sometimes JTAG is unreliable, or unsupported on the hardware. A reliable boot loader is a vital tool for systems engineering efforts. The software principles learned while creating a boot loader are perhaps the most important reason to create a UART based boot loader at this time. Where to put the executable binary data in RAM, and how to execute it once transferred from the development PC are very important concepts to know when creating software for hardware systems. If we just use JTAG and GDB to 'load' an ELF file, we never learn these details.

Additionally, the build and execute procedure of the development process should be quick and support rapid and incremental build and test cycles. With a boot loader usable from the development PC and integrated into the same shell used during interaction with the system software executable, the development cycle is simplified. TeraTerm (or ExtraPuTTY) for Windows or Minicom for Linux provide the ability to interact with the boot loader and transfer binary executables for testing.

7.2 Configure the Boot Loader

By default a bare metal application ('-ffreestanding') is linked so the first function of the first linked file is the default entry point (beginning of execution). This is why main.o has been, and is required to be, the first argument to the linker (arm-none-eabi-ld) command. The first goal of this section is to define an assembly entry point, named _start, so that we can control the start of execution as well as the starting stack address pointer. Let us review a simple 'app.s' assembly file that sets the stack pointer address and then branches to main(), the C software entry point. If this 'app.o' were linked first then 'main.o' could be linked in any order after it and the execution behavior would be the same as if 'main.o' were linked first with the additional benefit that we can now control the entry point as well as the stack pointer.

```
.globl _start
_start:
    mov sp, #0x01000000
    bl main
hang: b hang
```

This _start function initializes the stack pointer (sp) far away in the RAM memory (0x01000000) so as not to conflict with the binary executable already in memory (remember the binary begins at address 0x8000 because of the ORIGIN = 0x8000 line in the 'memory.map' file). The stack pointer is the location where local variables are stored as well as function parameters during execution. As software navigates into and out of functions, it is the stack in RAM that is used as the location to store local variables and function parameters. The stack pointer grows downward in RAM (toward the executable in RAM) as more local variables are declared and functions entered. After initializing the stack pointer, this assembly routine then branches to the C function main(), which is the beginning of the executable from a C language perspective. If main() returns, the hang loop is invoked, preventing system execution from continuing beyond this point, without halting execution so that JTAG remains active.

In the companion book we learned about boot loader design and the Xmodem protocol. The key to the design is to modify the assembly language _start entry point to create the empty space before calling main(). Written in assembly language, the typical _start entry point looks like the 'boards/rpi/app.s' created in the previous section. For the boot loader, a jump is needed at the beginning of _start, followed by a bunch of empty space and then the bootloader execution code. While the .globl keyword defines a global function, the .space keyword defines a range of memory to save for the program. The first argument to .space is the size, followed by the initialization value. Below is the bootloader startup initialization assembly language routine (loader.s). It fills the executable binary with zeros until near the 16MB location in RAM where the actual boot loader executable begins. This can be calculated by subtracting the 0x8000 start point and an additional 4 bytes for the branch instruction, represented in the 0x8004 below.

```
.globl _start
_start:
    b _skip

.space 0x01000000-0x8004,0

_skip:
    mov sp,#0x02000000
    bl main
_hang: b _hang
```

Let use create this assembly file 'board/rpi/loader.s' now. It is specific to the bootloader and moves the bootloaders main() and other functions away from the initial entry point. Please copy this assembly language source code above into this file. This code zeros the executable up to address 0x01000000, minus the 0x8000 start point and four bytes for the 'b skip' instruction. After this spacing is the true bootloader entry point of main(). Now that we have the bootloader executable high into RAM, the boot loader can safely write an executable in memory at the normal start point for the Raspberry Pi, address 0x8000. Doing so will overwrite the single 'b skip' instruction, but this is needed for the initial boot loader execution only. Note that the **boot loader** stack pointer address is twice the value as that of the application in app.s. It is desirable for the two stacks to stay out of each others way as this opens the possibility to using the boot loader as a simple debugger as it can access the application stack, without changing it.

7.3 Xmodem shell command

Now let us create the 'xmodem' shell command that uses XmodemDownload() to transfer data from the development PC to the execution starting point in RAM, or 0x8000. To aid portability to new systems let us define the RAM starting point in board.h for both the runtime executable where xmodem stores the transferred binary

(RUN_BASE_ADDR) and initializes the stack (RUN_STACK_ADDR) as well as the bootloaders base address (BOOT_BASE_ADDR) and stack address (BOOT_STACK_-ADDR).

```
#define RUN_BASE_ADDR   0x00008000 /* Base of new binary */
#define BOOT_BASE_ADDR  0x01000000 /* Base of bootloader binary */
```

Next create the new shell command 'xmodem', 'run' and 'quit' along with the associated functions xmodem(), run() and quit(). Finally register the commands with the shell by putting them into the ShellCommands[] array.

```
/*
** Shell Functions
*/
#if ENABLE_BOOTLOADER
static int xmodem(const char *command);
#endif
static int echo(const char *command);
static int led(const char *command);
static int run(const char *command);
static int quit(const char *command);

/*.....................................................................*/
/* Global Variables                                                    */
/*.....................................................................*/
static struct ShellCmd ShellCommands[] =
{
  {"echo", echo},
  {"ledon", led},
  {"ledoff", led},
#if ENABLE_BOOTLOADER
  {"xmodem", xmodem},
#endif
  {"run", run},
  {"exit", quit},
  {0, 0},
```

```
};

/*...................................................................*/
/* Local function definitions                                        */
/*...................................................................*/

/*...................................................................*/
/*    echo: Echo a string to all consoles                            */
/*                                                                   */
/*   input: command = the entire command                             */
/*                                                                   */
/*  return: 0                                                        */
/*...................................................................*/
static int echo(const char *command)
{
  /* Echo the command to the console. */
  puts(command);
  return 0;
}

/*...................................................................*/
/*     led: Command to turn the LED on or off                        */
/*                                                                   */
/*   input: command = the entire command                             */
/*                                                                   */
/*  return: 0                                                        */
/*...................................................................*/
static int led(const char *command)
{
  /* Check the last letter of the command */

  /* If 'ledon' then last array element 4 is 'n' */
  if (command[4] == 'n')
    LedOn();

  /* Otherwise if 'ledoff' then array element 4 is 'f' */
```

```
  else if (command[4] == 'f')
    LedOff();
  else
    UartPuts("error - shell mishandled command?");

  return 0;
}

#if ENABLE_BOOTLOADER
/*...................................................................*/
/*  xmodem: Perform the xmodem download and run command              */
/*                                                                   */
/*   input: command = the entire command                             */
/*                                                                   */
/*  return: 0                                                        */
/*...................................................................*/
static int xmodem(const char *command)
{
  int length;
  unsigned char *base = (unsigned char *)_run_location();
  u32 size = _run_size();

  /* Wait for an Xmodem download. */
   puts("Waiting for Xmodem to receive target image...");
  length = XmodemDownload(base, size);

  /* If data was downloaded report the status. */
  if (length > 0)
  {
    usleep(MICROS_PER_SECOND / 100); /* 1/100 second delay */
    if (length == size)
    {
      puts("Download failed, length exceeded maximum");
      puts("Increase the _run_size()");
    }
    else
```

```
    puts("Download complete, type 'run' to execute the application");
  }

  /* Otherwise report the failure. */
  else
  {
    if (length < 0)
      puts("Download failed");
    else
      puts("Download timed out");
  }

  /* Return command completion. */
  return 0;
}
#endif
```

Xmodem allows executables to be accurately and reliably transferred from the development PC to the Raspberry Pi. To transfer a new executable image first enter 'xmodem' in the system shell, causing the RPi to send a NAK every second while waiting for the development PC to send the executable file using TeraTerm or Minicom over the serial UART connection. Using one of these applications, select send and the Xmodem protocol and then choose the executable file and it will be transferred with the Xmodem protocol.

7.4 Run and quit shell commands

After transferring the executable image it must be executed. To accomplish this we first create an assembly function to be used by the 'run' shell command. Open 'boards/rpi/loader.s' and add the _branch_to_run() and _branch_to_boot() functions below. The branch function takes an address as the first parameter (saved as r0 by the compiler). This function provides a C language interface to an unconditional jump in the assembly language of the Raspberry Pi hardware. Please add this assembly function to the end of both 'boards/rpi/loader.s' and 'boards/rpi/app.s' files now.

```
;@ Set boot stack address and branch to BOOT_BASE_ADDR to execute
;@ bootloader.
.globl _branch_to_boot
_branch_to_boot:
    mov sp, #0x02000000
    mov r0, #0x01000000
    bx r0

;@ Set run stack address and branch to RUN_BASE_ADDR to execute
;@ application transferred to RAM with xmodem.
.globl _branch_to_run
_branch_to_run:
    mov sp, #0x01000000
    mov r0, #0x00008000
    bx r0
```

The next code step is to create the run() command to use the new assembly _branch function to jump to the default execution location.

```
/*.................................................................*/
/*     run: Exectute application                                   */
/*                                                                 */
/*   input: command = the entire command                           */
/*                                                                 */
/*  return: 0                                                      */
/*.................................................................*/
static int run(const char *command)
{
  /* Branch to the application. */
  _branch_to_run();
  return 0; /* not reached */
}
```

The final step is to create the quit() command to use the new assembly _branch function to jump back to the bootloader execution location. The quit() command will _branch the CPU execution to the beginning of the boot loader, to execute it again.

This will only work if the bootloader is designed to be executable multiple times with no pre-configuration, commonly known as re-entrant. The bootloader in this book has been designed to be reentrant, so let us add the code now.

```
/*.....................................................................*/
/*    quit: Perform the exit command                                   */
/*                                                                     */
/*   Input: command = the entire command                               */
/*                                                                     */
/*  return: 0                                                          */
/*.....................................................................*/
static int quit(const char *command)
{
  /* Branch to the bootloader. */
  _branch_to_boot();
  return 0; /* not reached */
}
```

Combine this new new source code together with the xmodem code from the companion book of the same chapter and compile and execute the boot loader. This boot loader with Xmodem protocol requires the development PC to have TeraTerm/ExtraPuTTY if Windows, or minicom if Linux, as these have xmodem protocol support. These applications have so many options they are confusing to the inexperienced. The next section will describe using the commands 'xmodem', 'run' and 'quit' to load, execute and reenter the boot loader using a client application running on the development PC.

7.5 Xmodem through the development PC

TeraTerm for Windows and Minicom for Linux are great system shell clients that support serial UART hardware and the Xmodem protocol. These are the recommended UART clients for use on the development PC.

TeraTerm sends files with the menu options File->Transfer->XMODEM->Send. This menu option opens a dialog box to choose the file to transfer. The procedure to transfer and execute a file is to call 'xmodem' in the system shell of the boot loader, then choose the menu option 'File->Transfer->XMODEM->Send' in TeraTerm and upon selection of the binary file previously compiled, it will be transferred. Then the 'run' command can then be used to execute the binary file previously transferred to memory with xmodem.

'Minicom' can send files by holding down the 'Ctrl-A' keys and then the 'Z' key to bring up the menu. Then choose 'S' for 'Send files' and select 'xmodem' from the list. Alternatively you can use 'Ctrl-A' and then 'S' directly, bypassing the menu. Then you will be able to use the file system and choose the executable to transfer. It is very annoying to navigate the file system in 'minicom' and often simpler to copy the .bin executable to your home directory before calling 'minicom' so that it is easy to get at using the primitive 'minicom' file system interface for 'xmodem'. Alternatively, the 'Ctrl-A' and then 'O' key will bring up the configuration screen. Select 'Filenames and paths', then press 'B' to change the 'Upload directory'. Then type in the complete path to the application you wish to transfer with Xmodem, such as '/home/pi/Lab7 Boot Loader/applications/console'. Then the Xmodem transfer will default to this directory when sending (uploading) with Xmodem.

7.6 Editing files and Building software with Geany

While the command line is a great interface to learn software creation, it can become a tedious interface when used for editing and compiling software day after day. It would be great to be able to open/edit source files and compile the software all from the same Windows or Linux application. The open source authors of Geany have created such an environment, providing a full featured editor and easy integration with Makefiles. Each source code application has its own project file that keeps track of the directories, files and Makefiles used for compiling. Once configured, compiling an application with Geany is a one click process.

What is 'Geany'? It is an advanced text editor designed for editing source code that includes compile, build and make integration. The home page for Geany is www.geany.org and has the latest version packaged for installation on Windows or Linux. From the development PC, please go to the geany.org website and download and install the latest 'Geany'. There are many features and configuration options with Geany that the reader can take advantage of. For example, there is a great Find in Files feature and the ability to set temporary markers in the code and then search for them later. For Debian based Linux development PC's Geany can be installed with 'sudo apt-get install geany'. Geany is installed by default with Raspbian.

The first step for the new Geany user is to find an editor style that is pleasing to you. Open 'Geany' and then open the main.c file for an application. Notice the color coding in the C file, highlighting the code portions is helpful when scanning source code with your eyes. The color scheme, as it is called, can be changed to the readers preference. From the 'View' menu, select 'Change Color Scheme'. A dialog will open with a list of different color schemes. On Raspbian the Default is recommended but there are more options so choose one which is appealing to you. You can change it at any time in the future. Unlike a word processor, the color scheme does not change the raw text in the source file. Instead Geany pre-compiles the source code when the file is opened, similar to the compiler, adding the colors for the configured color scheme. If you prefer dark background, like the author, the 'Edit' menu, 'Preferences' option opens a dialog box. In the 'Display' tab there is an "Invert syntax highlighting colors' check box that will invert the colors, including the background color. The author uses and recommends the 'Default' color scheme with inverted syntax.

With the editor configured it is time to create a project. From the Project menu select New. In the New Project dialog enter bootloader as the project Name and then change the project file location by clicking on the folder to the right of the Filename box. Navigate to the 'bootloader' application directory for this laboratory assignment (where the main.c is) and create the project file here. For the working directory, cut and paste the directory from the Filename above, without the project filename bootloader.geany. For example, '/home/pi/Lab7 Boot Loader/applications/bootloader' would be the directory and 'bootloader.geany' will be the project file that 'Geany' will create. Press the 'Create' button to create the project.

With a project created we can now configure the settings. In Project menu select Properties. In the dialog that opens, double check that the name, Filename and Base path are all correct and then select the Indentation tab. Set the Width to 2 and the Type to Spaces to follow the coding conventions used in this book. Then open the Files tab and turn on all the Saving files features. Finally, change the Build command to 'make' and then copy the project Base path (from Project tab) to the Working directory. Copy this directory to the working directory in all four Independent commands related to Make in the middle of the dialog. Click on the last command (blank 4) and change to Make _Clean, setting the command to 'make clean' and verifying the Working directory is set correctly. Finally, in the Execute commands, Execute section, add 'arm-none-eabi-gdb -tui bootloader.elf' and copy the base path to the working directory.

After these changes the Build button (or Build menu options) should Make the project and the Make Clean option should appear in the Build menu. With Make integrated into Geany, errors during compiling are output at the bottom of Geany, and clicking on the error will open the location within the file that has the error. The function button F8 will also build and holding down Alt and pressing B will open the Build menu, then the character C will execute the 'Make _Clean' option. It can be helpful to remember the hot keys so you can compile anytime using the keyboard. Alt-B and then 'M' to Make, while Alt-B and 'C' will Make Clean. Note that different OSs and Geany versions behave a bit differently so play around if something doesn't match the above description. To execute the created application, click the paper airplane icon or press Alt-B then 'E' (or the F5 key) shortcut. It is still required to run OpenOCD bit bang controller in another console window and connect to the remote target (target remote :3333) once GDB is started.

An important feature we leave to the user to investigate is the Search menu's Find in Files feature which can search entire directory trees if the 'Recurse in subfolders' option is selected. This can be used to search the entire source code tree. We hope you enjoy Geany as much as the author does, but if not, you are welcome to continue using the command line and your favorite editor, or any other IDE of your preference.

7.7 Cleaning up the RPi Boot Loader

One major concern for the future of the RPi bootloader is the use of constant addresses in many places that are either hard coded or defined for only subsections of the code. For example, the RUN_BASE_ADDR and BOOT_BASE_ADDR are defined in board.h but these cannot be used in pure assembly so they are duplicated in app.s. Even the linker script 'memory.map' uses these same hard coded addresses for the ORIGIN and LENGTH. The final effort of this chapter is to consolidate the fixed addresses into a single definition and use it throughout the code base. This is a simple concept but results in many changes.

The first decision made was to put the definitions into an assembly language file 'define.s'. In this file we define four things, the boot loader base address, boot loader **stack address**, run base address and run **stack address**. Using these four definitions we can derive all the other values and hopefully create a deeper understanding for the reader. Let us review this 'define.s' now.

```
RUN_BASE_ADDR    = 0x00008000; /* Base of new binary */
RUN_STACK_ADDR   = 0x01000000; /* Start of new binary stack */
BOOT_BASE_ADDR   = 0x01000000; /* Base of bootloader binary */
BOOT_STACK_ADDR = 0x02000000; /* Start of bootloader stack */
```

With these defined, the 'app.s' _start entry point can use these defines. Let us also expand this 'app.s' to re-execute the boot loader after main() exits, instead of the hang loop.

```
include "define.s"

globl _start
_start:
    mov sp, #RUN_STACK_ADDR
    bl main
    mov sp, #BOOT_STACK_ADDR
    mov r0, #BOOT_BASE_ADDR ;@ Branch to bootloader if main exits
    bx r0
```

Then the 'loader.s' becomes this.

```
.include "define.s"

.globl _start
_start:
    bl _skip

.space (BOOT_BASE_ADDR - (RUN_BASE_ADDR + 4)), 0

_skip:
    mov sp, #BOOT_STACK_ADDR
    bl main
    mov sp, #BOOT_STACK_ADDR
    mov r0, #BOOT_BASE_ADDR ;@ Branch to bootloader if main exits
    bx r0
```

The _branch_to_run() and _branch_to_boot() assembly functions are changed below to use the new 'define.s' definitions. Also the xmodem protocol has two additional values needed from the board, the location to put the executable, or _run_location(), as well as the greatest allowed size of the executable, or _run_size(). Let us create a new 'rpi.s' file with these functions now and add an '.include "rpi.s"' line at the bottom of both app.s and loader.s.

To return a value from an assembly function, the value should be put into the register 'r0', before branching with 'bx' to the returning function ('lr'). The 'lr' is the link register and is used to hold the return address for a function call.

```
;@ Set boot stack address and branch to BOOT_BASE_ADDR to execute
;@ bootloader.
.globl _branch_to_boot
_branch_to_boot:
    mov sp, #BOOT_STACK_ADDR
    mov r0, #BOOT_BASE_ADDR
    bx r0

;@ Set run stack address and branch to RUN_BASE_ADDR to execute
;@ application transferred to RAM with xmodem.
.globl _branch_to_run
_branch_to_run:
    mov sp, #RUN_STACK_ADDR
    mov r0, #RUN_BASE_ADDR
    bx r0

;@ Run location is the RUN_BASE_ADDR
.globl _run_location
_run_location:
    mov r0, #RUN_BASE_ADDR
    bx lr

;@ Run size is the boot base minus the run base
.globl _run_size
_run_size:
    mov r0, #BOOT_BASE_ADDR
```

```
    sub r0, #RUN_BASE_ADDR
    bx lr
```

Finally let us update the top of the 'memory.map' linker script with the definitions in 'define.s'.

```
INCLUDE ../../boards/rpi/define.s

MEMORY
{
    ram : ORIGIN = RUN_BASE_ADDR, LENGTH = RUN_STACK_ADDR
}
```

The final change is to update the xmodem() shell command so that it uses the new _run_location() and _run_size() functions created in 'rpi.s'.

```
/*...................................................................*/
/*  xmodem: Perform the xmodem download and run command              */
/*                                                                   */
/*    input: command = the entire command                            */
/*...................................................................*/
static int xmodem(const char *command)
{
  int length;
  unsigned char *base = (unsigned char *)_run_location();
  u32 size = _run_size();

  /* Wait for an Xmodem download. */
   puts("Waiting for Xmodem to receive target image...");
  length = XmodemDownload(base, size);
```

Lab 8: Periodically Executed Task Scheduler

8.1 Why an OS?

The system shell and bootloader created so far work without any known defect and it would be possible to use this software base to immediately add a Raspberry Pi GPU hardware interface to create a video console and graphical interface. Another software driver could be created to use the USB keyboard, mouse and even enable networking over the Internet. But to use all of these peripherals together efficiently requires an Operating System or OS. The goal of an operating system is to balance the execution of user applications and the servicing of peripherals. As the number of peripherals and user software increases, so does the need for an OS.

The primary reason for an operating system is to allow many applications and peripherals to coordinate and efficiently share the execution time of the SoC (CPU/G-PU/RAM). Operating systems share the CPU with applications by assigning each application as a **task** of a specific priority. If multiple tasks or peripherals must be serviced quickly (or data will be lost, etc.) an operating system is helpful. Creating a video frame or printing a UART string can delay the servicing of other peripherals or software. Only an OS can ensure that priority is enforced so that critical peripherals and tasks are serviced whenever ready.

Why not start with this design? Why did we design the previous system shell and bootloader without an OS and now have to change it? The goal of the previous chapters and laboratories was to create the simplest shell interface and bootloader possible. The operating system concept is difficult to understand so beginning with this would have only added complexity without solving any problems. Now that system shell, LED and Xmodem interfaces are available, it is simple to demonstrate the benefits of an operating system. An operating system is vital for the success of complex systems but most operating systems are more complex than the problems they solve. The intent of this laboratory is to minimize OS complexity by using a non-blocking **priority loop scheduler**.

The success of this design depends on how well each peripheral service routine and user application can be designed to execute as a non-blocking, **periodically executed** function call. This operating system design is a primitive software to hardware interface that can clearly expose the pre-emptive **operating system** paradigm. Modern pre-emptive **operating systems** were created to solve the problem of executing multiple monolithic algorithms at the same time. With manufacturers nearing the physical atomic limit for creating microscopic circuits and the software to hardware interface relatively unchanged in 40 years, the opportunity for disruptive computer systems is high. New hardware designs of the future, such as more and more hardware CPU cores, requires a new Operating System design if the speed and user experience is to continue to improve with the plateau in hardware transistor miniaturization.

Future improvements to this **priority loop operating system** could be interrupt processing, priority escalations and parallel processing for multi-core. Integrating the OS to the CPU sleep states in order to optimize battery use would also be a great future effort.

8.2 Speed up LED blink during shell command

A modification to the bootloader so that shell commands blink the LED 8 times a second while a command is executing is a great example of the abilities of the operating system. It is also a great debugging tool to detect since if a task execution introduces a noticeable delay, the LED will stop blinking. Observe the LED blink rate during shell command execution, a faster LED blinking ensures the shell command (xmodem, etc.) is in fact periodically executing and not hogging the OS or CPU. In ShellPoll() below, after activating the shell command we change the LedTime and reset the LedState expiration time.

```
/* If not an empty command then look up the command structure. */
else if (state->i)
{
  state->cmd = shell((char *)state->command);
  if (state->cmd == NULL)
  {
    state->puts("command unknown");
    state->result = TASK_FINISHED;
  }
  else
  {
    LedTime = LedTime / 8;
    LedState.expire = TimerRegister(LedTime);
    command_time = TimerNow();
  }
}
```

'Xmodem' is an existing command that can be used to verify that the LED state will blink rapidly while a command is executing. Alternatively or additionally, the reader can demonstrate the new feature with their own command to perform a long calculation or delay. Do not forget to slow the LED blink down to one second after the shell command complets in ShellPoll().

```
/* Calculate clock delta and return command result. */
command_time = TimerNow() - command_time;
putu32(command_time);

/* Restore led timer. */
LedTime = LedTime * 8;
LedState.expire = TimerRegister(LedTime);
```

8.3 Periodically executed Xmodem protocol

The 'xmodem' command waits for the sending and takes time to transfer. How to make this algorithm periodically executed is not trivial. The first step to change a task (shell command, etc.) to support periodic execution should always be is to create a structure containing the local variables. For 'xmodem' this would be the local variables from XmodemDownload(). The next step is to create a new function XmodemPoll() with a void pointer parameter that will be used to pass this Xmodem structure to the periodically executed XmodemPoll() function. In XmodemPoll(), remove the outer loop from XmodemDownload() and return 'finished' once the download completes or a timeout occurs. Replace the repurposed XmodemDownload() implementation with a loop calling XmodemPoll() so non-OS support is maintained. Compiling and executing these changes will not solve the problem however. Let us review the changes to the xmodem.c functions so far and try to spot the problem.

```
struct xmodem_state
{
  u8 *destination, packet[XMODEM_PACKET_SIZE];
  int block, rcvd, retry, i, length;
  struct timer packet_timer;
  struct shell_state *shell;
};

/*.................................................................*/
/* Globals                                                         */
/*.................................................................*/
struct xmodem_state XmodemState;

...

/*.................................................................*/
/* Global Functions                                                */
/*.................................................................*/

/*.................................................................*/
/*  XmodemInit: initialize the Xmodem channel                      */
/*                                                                 */
/*        Input: destination = location to save Xmodem data        */
/*               length = maximum length of Xmodem data            */
/*                                                                 */
```

```
/*     Returns: task state (TASK_IDLE, TASK_READY, TASK_FINISHED)   */
/*..................................................................*/
void *XmodemInit(unsigned char *destination, int length)
{
  /* Return failure if xmodem state is in use. */
  /* This could be replaced by a loop if multiple xmodems expected. */
  if (XmodemState.block)
    return NULL;

  /* Initialize the xmodem state. */
  XmodemState.block = 1;
  XmodemState.rcvd = XmodemState.retry = XmodemState.i = 0;
  XmodemState.destination = destination;
  XmodemState.length = length;
  XmodemState.shell = StdioState;

  return &XmodemState;
}

/*..................................................................*/
/*  XmodemPoll: poll the Xmodem download                            */
/*                                                                  */
/*       Input: data = pointer to Xmodem state                      */
/*                                                                  */
/*     Returns: task state (TASK_IDLE, TASK_READY, TASK_FINISHED)   */
/*..................................................................*/
int XmodemPoll(void *data)
{
  int result;
  struct xmodem_state *state = data;

  /* Check timer and process timeout if needed. */
  if (TimerExpired(state->packet_timer))
  {
    /* Break out if retry count exceeds maximum. */
    if (++state->retry > XMODEM_DATA_RETRY)
```

```
    {
      state->shell->puts("Timeout");

      /* Clear block to free Xmodem and return failure. */
      state->block = 0;
      return TASK_FINISHED;
    }

    /* Restart timer and index. */
    state->packet_timer = TimerRegister(XMODEM_DATA_TIMEO);
    state->i = 0;

    /* Send a NAK. */
    state->shell->putc(NAK);
  }

  /* Check if character is available to read. */
  if (state->shell->check())
  {
    /* Get the next character. */
    result = state->shell->getc();

    /* Check if first character of block. */
    if (state->i == 0)
    {
      /* Transfer success if first character is EOT. */
      if (result == EOT)
      {
        /* Received size, in blocks minus start and end frames. */
        state->rcvd = (state->block - 2) * XMODEM_PACKET_SIZE;

        /* Trim EOF markers from last frame and return length. */
        while ((state->rcvd > 0) &&
               (state->destination[state->rcvd - 1] == CPMEOF))
          --state->rcvd;
```

```
      /* Send ACK on xmodem transfer success. */
      state->shell->putc(ACK);

      /* Clear block to free Xmodem and return success. */
      state->block = 0;
      puts("Download complete,'run' to execute the application");
      return TASK_FINISHED;
    }
  }

  /* Save the character to the packet and increment count. */
  state->packet[state->i++] = result;

  /* Check if an entire packet has been collected. */
  if (state->i == XMODEM_PACKET_SIZE)
  {
    /* Process the xmodem packet and return the block offset. */
    result = process_xmodem(state->packet, state->block & 0xFF);

    /* If resulting block offset valid, save block. */
    if (result >= 0)
    {
      /* Preserve previous block overflows but adjust for resends. */
      state->block = result | (state->block & 0xFFFFFF00); /*  */

      /* Copy the xmodem frame to the destination buffer. */
      memcpy(
        &state->destination[(state->block - 1) * XMODEM_DATA_SIZE],
        &state->packet[XMODEM_PACKET_SIZE - XMODEM_DATA_SIZE - 1],
        XMODEM_DATA_SIZE);

      /* Increment received blocks and clear retry count. */
      ++state->block;

      /* Send ACK on success. */
      state->shell->putc(ACK);
```

```
      }
      else
      {
        /* On failure flush and send NAK. */
        state->shell->flush();
        state->shell->putc(NAK);
      }

      /* Restart the packet timer. */
      state->packet_timer = TimerRegister(XMODEM_DATA_TIMEO);

      /* Clear retry and position counters. */
      state->retry = state->i = 0;
    }
    return TASK_READY;
  }
  else
    return TASK_IDLE;
}

/*...................................................................*/
/* XmodemDownload: download and run an application using Xmodem     */
/*                                                                   */
/*       Input: timeout value                                        */
/*                                                                   */
/*     Returns: length of download on success, or -1 if error        */
/*...................................................................*/
int XmodemDownload(unsigned char *destination, int length)
{
  struct xmodem_state *state;

  /* Initialize xmodem for this transfer, returning if error. */
  state = XmodemInit(destination, length);
  if (state == NULL)
    return -1;
```

```
  /* Loop that polls Xmodem until it finishes. */
  for (;XmodemPoll(state) != TASK_FINISHED;) ;

  /* Clear Xmodem state for other tasks and return download length. */
  state->block = 0;
  return state->rcvd;
}
```

Now that Xmodem has a periodically executable "poll" function, there is one final change needed to the shell implementation to support it. Instead of calling XmodemDownload() it must save the command state and call XmodemPoll(). Every subsequent execution of the shell task will check the command state and if a command is in progress it will call the registered poll function (XmodemPoll()) instead of checking the UART input for the next command. To achieve this the shell must be able to save the commands' polled function and pointer to its state variable. The shell task saves the function and data pointers when the command is initiated and calls these for every poll of the shell until the command completes. Let us review the shell.c code changes now to the xmodem() command now.

```
#if ENABLE_XMODEM
/*...................................................................*/
/*  xmodem: Perform the xmodem download and run command              */
/*                                                                   */
/*   input: command = the entire command                             */
/*                                                                   */
/*  return: TASK_IDLE if in progress, TASK_FINISHED if complete      */
/*...................................................................*/
void *XmodemData;
static int xmodem(const char *command)
{
  int status;

  if (XmodemData == NULL)
  {
    puts("Waiting for Xmodem to receive target image...");
    XmodemData = XmodemStart((u8 *)_run_location(), _run_size());
```

```
    if (XmodemData == NULL)
    {
      puts("Xmodem already in progress, please try again later");
      return TASK_FINISHED;
    }
  }

  /* Periodic execution of the xmodem transfer. */
  status = XmodemPoll(XmodemData);
  if (status == TASK_FINISHED)
    XmodemData = NULL;
  return status;
}
#endif /* ENABLE_XMODEM */
```

Now the xmodem() shell callback function is periodically executed because it calls XmodemPoll(), which is periodically executable. Now the LED should blink quickly during the xmodem transfer and return to the one second blink rate once the command is complete and the shell command prompt reappears.

8.4 Comparing Source Code

Often it is desirable to compare different versions of software, for example the differences between chapters in this book. An open source application is available to do this named 'Meld'. 'Meld' is better at merging that comparing, but is the best open source option at this time. On Linux development systems 'Meld' can be installed with 'sudo apt-get install meld'. Windows development systems will need to search the web and install it, or BeyondCompare a commercial product focused on comparing. Be sure to get the binary from the official Meld website at meldmerge.org to avoid downloading an unofficial version that may have ad/spyware.

Use the 'Meld' application to compare the Lab7 and Lab8 directories. Navigate through all directories, opening and comparing files that are different. Comparing the application and system software changes highlights the incremental steps taken to achieve the next step. Systems engineering should be a careful incremental process, since the simplest mistake can break everything. Compare other adjacent Lab folders folders, such as Lab6 and Lab7 and any others of interest to the reader.

8.5 Dynamic tasks

It is helpful for applications and system software to be able to create new tasks during runtime. The goal of this section is to remove the global task array and create a TaskNew() command to replace it. TaskNew() returns the resulting task priority or less than zero if the call failed. Assume only one task can exist at the same priority at a time and there are 10 available tasks with priority 0 through 9, zero (0) being the highest priority.

If this function should maintain an array of tasks (up to a maximum) in order of priority, the TaskNew() can index into the task array with the priority. The TaskNew() command should have one parameter, a pointer to the task structure with the priority number already assigned. If a task of that priority is already present, TaskNew() should return an error. The application can detect this error and try again with a different priority if desired. If the USE_DYNAMIC_PRIORITY is TRUE, TaskNew() will automatically increase the priority and try again and will only return an error if no task is available.

The new functions TaskNew() and TaskEnd() below are added to os.c so that tasks can be managed by future applications and system software.

```
/*...........................................................*/
/* Configuration                                              */
/*...........................................................*/
#define USE_DYNAMIC_PRIORITY    TRUE /* true to increase priority  */
                                     /* until a task is available. */

...

/*...........................................................*/
/*    TaskNew: Create a new task                              */
/*                                                            */
/*      Input: priority the importance of the task            */
/*             poll the function to execute for the new task  */
```

```
/*              data is the state data structure for the new task     */
/*                                                                     */
/*    Returns: the resulting priority or less than zero if error      */
/*.....................................................................*/
int TaskNew(int priority, int (*poll) (void *data), void *data)
{
  /* Return if priority greater than allowed */
  if (priority >= MAX_TASKS)
  {
    puts("NewTask failed: priority greater than maximum.");
    return -1;
  }

#if USE_DYNAMIC_PRIORITY
  /* Increase (lower) priority until a task is available */
  /* if poll is NULL but data valid the task is disabled so skip */
  while ((Tasks[priority].poll != NULL) &&
         (Tasks[priority].data != NULL))
  {
    if (++priority >= MAX_TASKS)
    {
      puts("NewTask failed: non availble, including higher priority.");
      return -1;
    }
  }
#endif

  /* Set up the task to poll and return success */
  Tasks[priority].data = data;
  Tasks[priority].poll = poll;
  return priority;
}

/*.....................................................................*/
/*    TaskEnd: End an existing task                                   */
/*                                                                     */
```

```
/*      Input: priority the importance of the task                      */
/*                                                                       */
/*    Returns: the priority or less than zero if error                  */
/*.......................................................................*/
int TaskEnd(int priority)
{
  /* Return if priority greater than allowed or not in use */
  if ((priority >= MAX_TASKS) || (Tasks[priority].poll == NULL))
    return -1;

  /* Remove the polling for this task and return success */
  Tasks[priority].data = NULL;
  Tasks[priority].poll = NULL;
  return priority;
}
```

Lab 9: Video Screen

9.1 Why a Video Screen?

The video **screen** of a PC is the primary human interface. For young software creators, the video **screen** is a wonderful place to explore algorithms as creators can visually see the incremental changes and mistakes in their algorithms. The visual capabilities of the RPI can be used to provide a foundation for future creation. It must not be understated how important learning from mistakes are to the process of becoming a software creator. The creation experience is similar between software languages, but learning to detect mistakes, or debugging experience, is different for each compiled language such as C.

When software creators draw on the video screen, a new world of fun opportunities to learn and explore software creation become available. How a CPU communicates with the GPU to display images on the screen with the Raspberry Pi was in high demand by young readers of this book. Once the reader understands the details and interface to the **video screen**, the reader can move on to other more immediate interests, such as game development. A **video screen** is an open canvas for the software creator to explore algorithms such as geometry and math curves.

9.2 Mail Box Interface

The software to hardware interface to the video screen of the RPI is the mail box. The RPI mail box hardware interface is a collection of registers starting at offset 0xB880 from the RPI peripheral base address. The three registers for this simplified software interface provide operations for Read, Status and Write. A write is always first performed for a mail box transaction. When writing to an RPI mail box, both a channel and data pointer must be provided. The mail box interface uses only 32 bits of the RAM addresses, even in the CPU is 64 bit (RPI 3) as the GPU is 32 bits. The function write_read() below performs a complete transaction with the mail box software interface.

```
// Mailbox register map
#define MAILBOX_BASE    (PERIPHERAL_BASE + 0xB880)
#define MAILBOX_READ      MAILBOX_BASE
#define MAILBOX_STATUS    (MAILBOX_BASE + 0x18)
  #define MAILBOX_STATUS_EMPTY  (1 << 30)
  #define MAILBOX_STATUS_FULL   (1 << 31)
#define MAILBOX_WRITE     (MAILBOX_BASE + 0x20)

// Static local functions

/*..................................................................*/
/* flush: wait for all mailboxes to complete                        */
/*                                                                  */
/*..................................................................*/
void flush(void)
{
  // Read from the mailbox until status is empty
  while (!(REG32(MAILBOX_STATUS) & MAILBOX_STATUS_EMPTY))
    REG32(MAILBOX_READ);
}

/*..................................................................*/
/*      write: Write data to a mailbox channel                      */
/*                                                                  */
/*      Input: channel to write to                                  */
/*             data to write                                        */
/*                                                                  */
/*..................................................................*/
void write(u32 channel, uintptr_t data)
{
  // Read the mailbox status until it is not full
  while (REG32(MAILBOX_STATUS) & MAILBOX_STATUS_FULL) ;

  // Add the channel number before writing the data to mailbox.
  REG32(MAILBOX_WRITE) = channel | data;
}
```

```
/*....................................................................*/
/*      read: Read data from a mailbox channel                        */
/*                                                                    */
/*      Input: channel to read from                                   */
/*                                                                    */
/*     Return: data read from channel                                 */
/*....................................................................*/
u32 read(u32 channel)
{
  u32 result;

  // Read the mailbox until a result for this channel.
  for (result = REG32(MAILBOX_READ); (result & 0xF) != channel;
       result = REG32(MAILBOX_READ))
  {
    // Read the mailbox status until it is not empty
    while (REG32(MAILBOX_STATUS) & MAILBOX_STATUS_EMPTY);
  }

  // Return the result
  return result;
}

/*....................................................................*/
/* write_read: Write and then read data to/from a mailbox channel     */
/*                                                                    */
/*      Input: channel to read/write from/to                          */
/*             data to write                                          */
/*                                                                    */
/*     Return: data read from channel                                 */
/*....................................................................*/
static u32 write_read(u32 channel, uintptr_t data)
{
  u32 result;
```

```
  // Flush all before writing to the mailbox
  flush();
  write(channel, data);

  // Read and return mailbox result
  result = read(channel);

  // Output error if result of read does not match write channel
  if ((result & 0x0F) != channel)
    puts("Read channel does not match write!");

  // Return the result of read after removing the channel
  return result & ~0x0F;
}
```

On the RPI and most other systems the CPU and GPU share the same RAM and can use the mail box to share pointers to data in RAM. When using the mail box to communicate a pointer address with the GPU, it is important to have the GPU_-MEM_BASE flag added to the pointer address before writing to the mailbox. And remove the flag if reading a pointer from the mail box. Memory domain flags such as this help the CPU and GPU from share the same RAM while staying out of each others way. GPU_MEM_BASE flags the memory address as within the GPU domain otherwise the GPU will not access the RAM address.

```
  // Add the GPU memory base to the address and write the mailbox,
  // reading back the result, which will match the write if success
  bufferAddress = GPU_MEM_BASE + (u32)propBuffer;
  if (write_read(MAILBOX_PROPERTY_TAGS_OUT, bufferAddress) !=
                                                          bufferAddres\
s)
    return -1;
```

9.3 Property Tags

The VideoCore GPU communicates information in the form of property tags. These property tags can be chained together and sent through the mail box. We must now create a function to perform the complete property tag round trip transaction. Since this function is only needed internally it will be declared as a local static function and take two parameters, a pointer to the property and the size of the property. The property pointer must not be NULL and the property size must not be zero.

Aside from adding the GPU_MEM_BASE already mentioned above, it is also required that the mail box buffer pointer be 16 byte aligned. To align an address by 16 bytes requires declaring a buffer larger than necessary and then adjusting the starting address of the buffer so that the address is a multiple of 16, which aligns the address to 16 bytes. This alignment is needed so the channel can be added to the pointer during a write() to the mail box.

Once a 16 byte aligned buffer is available the property_get() function then creates a property buffer with code request (CODE_REQUEST) and the buffer size before copying the property to the new aligned buffer. Finally we add the end tag (u32 integer of value zero) to the end of the buffer, the GPU_MEM_BASE flag to the buffer address, and write the whole thing to the mailbox.

```
// Mailbox channels
#define CHANNEL_PROPERTY_TAGS_OUT       8

// Property buffer codes
#define CODE_REQUEST                    0x00000000
#define CODE_RESPONSE_SUCCESS           0x80000000
#define CODE_RESPONSE_FAILURE           0x80000001

typedef struct PropertyBuffer
{
  u32 bufferSize;
  u32 code;
  u8  property[0];
}
PropertyBuffer;
```

```
typedef struct PropertyTag
{
  u32 tagId;
  u32 bufSize;
  u32 code;
}
PropertyTag;

...

/*..................................................................*/
/* property_get: Write and then read through property tag interface  */
/*                                                                   */
/*      Input: property is a pointer to the data to write/read       */
/*             propertySize is the size of the property              */
/*                                                                   */
/*     Return: zero (0) on success, negative value on error          */
/*..................................................................*/
static int property_get(void *property, u32 propertySize)
{
  // Determine length of property buffer based on the tag size
  u32 bufferSize = sizeof(PropertyBuffer) + propertySize + sizeof(u32);
  // Declare buffer with additional 15 bytes for alignment
  u8 buffer[bufferSize + 15];
  // Adjust pointer so that it is exactly 16 byte aligned
  PropertyBuffer *propBuffer =
                        (PropertyBuffer *)(((u32)buffer + 15) & ~15);
                                    /* __attribute__((aligned(16))) */
  u32 *endTag, bufferAddress;

  // Initialize with size, request code and copy tags
  propBuffer->bufferSize = bufferSize;
  propBuffer->code = CODE_REQUEST;
  memcpy(propBuffer->property, property, propertySize);
```

```
  // End the property tag
  endTag = (u32 *)(propBuffer->property + propertySize);
  *endTag = 0;

  // Add the GPU memory base to the address and write the mailbox,
  // reading back the result, which will match the write if success
  bufferAddress = GPU_MEM_BASE | (u32)propBuffer;
  if (write_read(CHANNEL_PROPERTY_TAGS_OUT, bufferAddress) !=
                                                      bufferAddress)
  {
    puts("write_read() failed");
    return -1;
  }

  // Check response and return failure if not success
  if (propBuffer->code != CODE_RESPONSE_SUCCESS)
  {
    puts("Property buffer code is not response");
    return -1;
  }

  // Copy property tag result to tag parameter and return success
  memcpy(property, propBuffer->property, propertySize);
  return 0;
}
```

9.4 Multiple Property Tags

The PropertyBuffer must end with the endTag of zero. This endTag, and the PropertyBuffer length, allow the interface to support more than one PropertyTag per PropertyBuffer. In fact, the RPi frame buffer interface requires multiple property tags in a single transaction to create the frame buffer. The frame buffer creation requires four (4) property tags, the physical resolution (width, height), the virtual resolution , the color depth and the resulting frame buffer address and size. The physical and virtual resolutions should be the same for our uses, and can be zero to read back the hardware auto negotiated settings. The color depth must be 16 or 32 and represents the bits per pixel, or bpp. The bufferAddr and bufferSize must be zero and are filled in by the GPU upon success. Any of the values, especially zero values, may be modified by the GPU during the **transaction** and the change in value is made to the property tag data structure in memory.

```
// Display
#define TAG_ALLOCATE_BUFFER              0x00040001
#define TAG_RELEASE_BUFFER               0x00048001
#define TAG_BLANK_SCREEN                 0x00040002
#define TAG_GET_PHYSICAL_WIDTH_HEIGHT 0x00040003
#define TAG_SET_PHYSICAL_WIDTH_HEIGHT 0x00048003
#define TAG_GET_VIRTUAL_WIDTH_HEIGHT  0x00040004
#define TAG_SET_VIRTUAL_WIDTH_HEIGHT  0x00048004
#define TAG_GET_BUFFER_DEPTH             0x00040005
#define TAG_SET_BUFFER_DEPTH             0x00048005
#define TAG_GET_BUFFER_PITCH             0x00040008

...

// Must include all display property tags in one mailbox transaction
typedef struct PropertyDisplayDimensions
{
  PropertyTag pTag; // Physical
  u32 pWidth;
  u32 pHeight;
  PropertyTag vTag; // Virtual
  u32 vWidth;
  u32 vHeight;
  PropertyTag dTag; // Depth
  u32 depth;
  PropertyTag fTag; // Framebuffer
  u32 bufferAddr;
  u32 bufferSize;
}
PropertyDisplayDimensions;
```

```
..

/*......................................................................*/
/* SetDisplayResolution: Write new framebuffer properties              */
/*                                                                      */
/*      Input: width is screen width (X)                               */
/*             height is screen height (Y)                             */
/*             depth is color depth (bpp)                              */
/*     Output: bufferAddr is a pointer to the framebuffer              */
/*                                                                      */
/*     Return: Framebuffer size on success, zero if error              */
/*......................................................................*/
u32 SetDisplayResolution(u32 *width, u32 *height, u32 *depth,
                         u32 *bufferAddr)
{
  PropertyDisplayDimensions dimensions;

  dimensions.pTag.tagId = TAG_SET_PHYSICAL_WIDTH_HEIGHT;
  dimensions.pTag.bufSize = 8; // 4 bytes each width and height
  dimensions.pTag.code = CODE_REQUEST;
  dimensions.pWidth = *width;
  dimensions.pHeight = *height;

  dimensions.vTag.tagId = TAG_SET_VIRTUAL_WIDTH_HEIGHT;
  dimensions.vTag.bufSize = 8; // 4 bytes each width and height
  dimensions.vTag.code = CODE_REQUEST;
  dimensions.vWidth = *width;
  dimensions.vHeight = *height;

  dimensions.dTag.tagId = TAG_SET_BUFFER_DEPTH;
  dimensions.dTag.bufSize = 4; // 4 bytes depth
  dimensions.dTag.code = CODE_REQUEST;
  dimensions.depth = *depth;

  dimensions.fTag.tagId = TAG_ALLOCATE_BUFFER;
```

```
  dimensions.fTag.bufSize = 8; // 4 bytes each addr and size
  dimensions.fTag.code = CODE_REQUEST;
  dimensions.bufferAddr = 0;
  dimensions.bufferSize = 0;

  // If success then assign the height and width output parameters
  if (property_get(&dimensions, sizeof(dimensions)) == 0)
  {
    // If resolution unspecified or allocation matches
    if (!*width || !*height || ((dimensions.pWidth == *width) &&
        (dimensions.pHeight == *height) &&
        (dimensions.vWidth == *width) &&
        (dimensions.vHeight == *height) &&
        (dimensions.depth == *depth)))
    {
      // Assign width, height, depth and buffer address, returning size
      *width  = dimensions.pWidth;
      *height = dimensions.pHeight;
      *depth = dimensions.depth;
      *bufferAddr = dimensions.bufferAddr;
      return dimensions.bufferSize;
    }

    // Otherwise out of sync so report an error
    else
      puts("ERROR framebuffer not valid\n");
  }

  // Otherwise zero the height and width output parameters
  else
    puts("set display resolution property failed");

  // Return failure
  return 0;
}
```

If the resolution and depth matches what was assigned then the software returns the resolution, depth and most importantly, the frame buffer address.

9.5 Framebuffer

The final step is to create the RPi **frame buffer** interface needed for the screen. Starting with declaring the VirdoCoreFrameBuffer structure, the FrameBufferNew() function is added that locates a free VideoCoreFrameBuffer and returns a void pointer to it. Then the Open() and Close() functions are created that initialize or clear the frame buffer resolution and color depth.

```
#if ENABLE_VIDEO

#define MAX_FRAMES 1

typedef struct VideoCoreFrameBuffer
{
  u32 width;       // Physical width of display in pixel
  u32 height;      // Physical height of display in pixel
  u32 virtWidth;   // same as physical width
  u32 virtHeight;  // same as physical height
  u32 depth;       // Number of bits per pixel (bpp)
  u32 bufferAddr;  // Address of frame buffer
  u32 bufferSize;  // Size of frame buffer
}
VideoCoreFrameBuffer;

typedef struct
{
  u8 align[16];
  VideoCoreFrameBuffer vcfb;
} Frame;
Frame Frames[MAX_FRAMES];

int FrameIndex = 0;
```

```
extern int FrameBufferIndex;

/*.................................................................*/
/* FrameBufferInit: Initialize the frame buffer interface         */
/*                                                                 */
/*.................................................................*/
void FrameBufferInit(void)
{
  FrameIndex = 0;
  FrameBufferIndex = 0;
}

/*.................................................................*/
/* FrameBufferNew: Allocate a new framebuffer structure           */
/*                                                                 */
/*     Return: pointer to framebuffer on success, NULL on error    */
/*.................................................................*/
void *FrameBufferNew(void)
{
  void *frame;

  // Return error (NULL) if no more frames available
  if (FrameIndex >= MAX_FRAMES)
    return NULL;

  // Zero out the frame
  bzero(&Frames[FrameIndex], sizeof(Frame));

  // 16 byte bus align the frame pointer
  frame = (void *)(((uintptr_t)&Frames[FrameIndex]) +
                   (16 - (((uintptr_t)&Frames[FrameIndex]) & 15)));

  // Increment frame index and return aligned frame pointer
  FrameIndex++;
  return frame;
}
```

```
/*...............................................................*/
/* FrameBufferClose: Close/Deallocate a framebuffer              */
/*                                                               */
/*      Input: fb is a pointer to the framebuffer                */
/*                                                               */
/*...............................................................*/
void FrameBufferClose(void *fb)
{
  VideoCoreFrameBuffer *frame = fb;

  bzero(frame, sizeof(VideoCoreFrameBuffer));
}

/*...............................................................*/
/* FrameBufferOpen: Open the framebuffer                         */
/*                                                               */
/*      Input: fb is a pointer to the framebuffer                */
/*             width is the screen width or X                    */
/*             height is the screen height or Y                  */
/*             depth is the color depth in bpp                   */
/*                                                               */
/*...............................................................*/
void FrameBufferOpen(void *fb, int width, int height, u32 depth)
{
  VideoCoreFrameBuffer *frame = fb;

  frame->width = width;
  frame->height = height;
  frame->virtWidth  = width;
  frame->virtHeight = height;
  frame->depth      = depth;
  frame->bufferAddr = 0;
  frame->bufferSize = 0;
}
```

Once the frame buffer is opened in can be initialized, which performs the SetDisplayResolution() step that will perform the mail box transaction and return a frame buffer address. Upon completion, the frame buffer is ready for use.

```
/*..............................................................*/
/* FrameBufferInitialize: Initialize the framebuffer            */
/*                                                              */
/*      Input: fb is a pointer to the framebuffer               */
/*                                                              */
/*     Return: zero (0) on success, negative value on error     */
/*..............................................................*/
int FrameBufferInitialize(void *fb)
{
  VideoCoreFrameBuffer *frame = fb;

  // Allocate framebuffer through mailbox to GPU
  frame->bufferSize = SetDisplayResolution(&frame->width,
                  &frame->height, &frame->depth, &frame->bufferAddr);

  // Ensure framebuffer is valid, return error if not
  if ((frame->bufferSize == 0) || (frame->bufferAddr == 0))
  {
    puts("Framebuffer create/set resolution failed");
    return -1;
  }

  // Return success
  return 0;
}
```

The last part of the frame buffer interface is to support the GetWidth(), GetHeight(), GetDepth(), GetBuffer() and GetSize() functions. Since the board specific frame buffer code only knows how to reference the VideoCoreFrameBuffer structure, these functions do that and pass back the associated frame buffer data. One thing worth pointing out is the removal of the GPU memory base (& ~GPU_MEM_BASE) from the frame buffer address. This base is required when the GPU is referencing the address but MUST be removed if the CPU is to reference the same memory address.

```
/*...................................................................*/
/* FrameBufferGetWidth: Return the width of the framebuffer          */
/*                                                                   */
/*      Input: fb is a pointer to the framebuffer                    */
/*                                                                   */
/*     Return: Width in pixels                                       */
/*...................................................................*/
u32 FrameBufferGetWidth(void *fb)
{
  VideoCoreFrameBuffer *frame = fb;

  return frame->width;
}

/*...................................................................*/
/* FrameBufferGetHeight: Return the height of the framebuffer        */
/*                                                                   */
/*      Input: fb is a pointer to the framebuffer                    */
/*                                                                   */
/*     Return: Height in pixels                                      */
/*...................................................................*/
u32 FrameBufferGetHeight(void *fb)
{
  VideoCoreFrameBuffer *frame = fb;

  return frame->height;
}

/*...................................................................*/
/* FrameBufferGetDepth: Return the color depth of the framebuffer    */
/*                                                                   */
/*      Input: fb is a pointer to the framebuffer                    */
/*                                                                   */
/*     Return: Depth in bits per pixel (bpp)                         */
/*...................................................................*/
u32 FrameBufferGetDepth(void *fb)
```

```
{
  VideoCoreFrameBuffer *frame = fb;

  return frame->depth;
}

/*.................................................................*/
/* FrameBufferGetBuffer: Return ARM relative RAM address of buffer   */
/*                                                                 */
/*      Input: fb is a pointer to the framebuffer                  */
/*                                                                 */
/*     Return: Framebuffer memory address (ie pointer to framebuffer)*/
/*.................................................................*/
u32 FrameBufferGetBuffer(void *fb)
{
  VideoCoreFrameBuffer *frame = fb;

  return frame->bufferAddr & ~GPU_MEM_BASE;
}

/*.................................................................*/
/* FrameBufferGetSize: Return size of framebuffer                  */
/*                                                                 */
/*      Input: fb is a pointer to the framebuffer                  */
/*                                                                 */
/*     Return: Framebuffer length in bytes                         */
/*.................................................................*/
u32 FrameBufferGetSize(void *fb)
{
  VideoCoreFrameBuffer *frame = fb;

  return frame->bufferSize;
}

#endif /* ENABLE_VIDEO */
```

9.7 Screen

Now that we have the underlying framebuffer supported for the RPI it is time to compile it together with the screen system designed in the companion book. Congratulations on initializing and using a framebuffer through the created screen interface.

Lab 10: Video Console

10.1 Why a Video Console?

For new software creators, displaying text on the video screen might seem a low priority when exploring how to display things on the screen with software. Graphs and windows would be much more fun, and the console through the UART are good arguments against the immediate need for a video console. Regardless of need, the video console is an excellent example of how to understand and create an interactive screen.

By organizing letters on the screen as a grid of cursor positions, the video console is the learning prerequisite for understanding windowing, games or any other complex use of the video screen. With letters as stamps of the same size, and the screen partitioned into a grid of these letters, the video screen can become a video console.

10.2 Font Map

A fixed size binary font map, in C source code form, is required for a console. We hope the reader has the time to create every letter of a font map from graph paper and calculating the hexadecimal. However, this would distract from the other concepts this chapter is trying to introduce. What we can do instead is leverage the work of others who have put their work in the public domain. One cool project in the public domain is uGUI by Achim Dobler (http://embeddedlightning.com/ugui/).

This project is a great place to read the source code for Graphical User Interfaces and goes way beyond this chapter or book. However, one small part of this project is a font map. There are many font maps in fact, but for this book we are going to use a fixed width 8x14 font map. Fixed width means that every letter has the same width in pixels. A fixed width font greatly simplifies the software we need to create and is the best starting place.

So let us now copy all the displayable characters from the uGUI 8x14 binary font map to a new character.c file. The file begins with definitions for the character width, height and also contains an extra height definition to allow extra spacing between lines. To complete this character.c file we need to provide an interface for returning the width, height and to check a character pixel bit in the map.

```
#define CHARACTER_WIDTH        8
#define CHARACTER_HEIGHT       14
#define CHARACTER_EXTRA_HEIGHT 6

static const u8 font_data[][CHARACTER_HEIGHT] = {
{0x00,0x00,0x00,0x00,0x00,0x00,0x00,
 0x00,0x00,0x00,0x00,0x00,0x00,0x00},   // 0x20
...
{0x00,0x00,0x00,0x00,0x00,0x86,0x99,
 0x61,0x00,0x00,0x00,0x00,0x00,0x00},   // 0x7E

u32 CharacterWidth()
{
  return CHARACTER_WIDTH;
}

u32 CharacterHeight()
{
  return CHARACTER_HEIGHT + CHARACTER_EXTRA_HEIGHT;
}

int CharacterPixel(char ascii, u32 x, u32 y)
{
  u32 fontbit;

  // Ensure x and y inputs are within the valid font size
  if (y >= CHARACTER_HEIGHT)
  {
    return 0;
  }
  if (x >= CHARACTER_WIDTH)
  {
```

```
    return 0;
  }

  // Shift font bit left based on character width
  // Framebuffer and font map are little endian, so first pixel is low
  // (bit zero or ((1 << 7) >> CHARACTER_WIDTH) and as x increases to
  // higher bits until 7 ((1 << 7) << 0).
  fontbit = ((1 << 7) >> (CHARACTER_WIDTH - x));

  // Reference this bit in the font data based on the ascii and y,
  // the particular character within the font map. Return if font bit
  // set or not.
  return ((font_data[(int)ascii][y] & fontbit) > 0 ? 1 : 0);
}
```

Hopefully the comments explain the code above. One complex part of the code above is that the font bit map is in mirror image, or stamp, format so the bits need to be unrolled when checking. So instead of starting at bit zero (0) and shift 1 bit for each x pixel, we need to start at the end bit (bit 7 or (1 << 7)) and shift a decreasing amount (CHARACTER_WIDTH - x). It might help to review this picture of the bits representing the open parenthesis character, unrolled to pixels.

```
{ 0x60, 0x30, 0x8, 0x8, 0x4, 0x4, 0x4,
  0x4, 0x4, 0x8, 0x8, 0x30, 0x60, 0x0 }, // 0x28 '('
```

Binary	Pixels
01100000	.....XX.
00110000	....XX..
00001000	...X....
00001000	...X....
00000100	..X.....
00000100	..X.....
00000100	..X.....
00000100	..X.....
00000100	..X.....
00001000	...X....
00001000	...X....

Binary	Pixels
00110000	....XX..
01100000	.....XX.
00000000	....

It is recommended the details of the font map stay inside the font map and not leak to the system software interface. A common font interface allows the system interface to add and use different **font maps** with little change.

10.3 Color conversion

The RPi VideoCore GPU requires 32 bit ARGB color format, while the system interface is 32 bit RGBA. The following Color32() function must be provided by board.c in order to work with the system software.

```
// RPI color interface is true color (32 bit ARGB)
//   Function must translate RGBA inputs into ARGB value for RPI
u32 Color32(u8 red, u8 green, u8 blue, u8 alpha)
{
    return (((blue) & 0xFF) | ((green) & 0xFF) << 8 |
            ((red) & 0xFF) << 16 | ((alpha) & 0xFF) << 24);
}
```

10.4 Binary Images

In the next chapter we create a virtual world, small steps at a time. To focus on the game logic next chapter, lets apply what we learned above about font maps and get a head start for next chapter. First, we will be using prior art images for the game, created and shared by Denzi under a Creative Commons license (CC BY-SA). How these pictures are converted to source code can also be applied to font maps. Learning binary bit maps allows the software creator to apply that knowledge when creating their own game. Similar to a font map, software must be able to reference individual pictures within the larger image, and then draw those individual images to the screen. The term bit map is officially introduced next chapter so if this is confusing to you please jump ahead to next chapters glossary and read the definition before continuing.

The Denzi tiles are a good starting point because they are binary (black and white) and there is a variety of terrain, structure, equipment, character, and creature tiles, each 16x16 pixels. The single Denzi picture (http://www3.wind.ne.jp/DENZI/diary/Denzi140330-12.png) is itself a collection of smaller pictures. The original was then cut and pasted, with Gimp, into three smaller images that contain certain groups of images, specifically items, creatures as well as terrain and players. Each image subset should be saved as an individual JPEG (jpg) so that it can be used in the next step. Gimp is a good tool to learn for creating and editing pictures and is the tool used by the author to create the book cover.

```
$ sudo apt install gimp
```

Using 'gimp' to create three subsets of the original, these three images are then processed by an image to C hex converter and stored as three arrays of hexadecimal u8 values in denzi_data.c. EquipmentData, CreatureData, and the TerrainCharactersData bitmaps. The image to C hex converter used was the free web interface (http://digole.com/tools/PicturetoC_Hex_converter.php) using the default settings, although there are other software products that can also convert an image to source code (hex, comma delimited) that represents a binary bit map. The goal is to reduce the size and add organization by splitting up the original image described previously. A modularized interface to the artwork can aid contributors.

The byte array output should be cut and pasted from the web converter to the denzi_-data.c file and then compiled into the application. Afterward, each individual image in the byte array can be referenced with a location index, similar to how the ASCII code is used to find characters in the font map. For ease of reading the code we will define the image index's to a name that best describes that image. The software interface must be able to look up the individual bits of each tile, and the tile number index algorithm needs to know how many tiles are in each row. These index values are bit map specific and the three bit map data variables are TerrainCharactersData, CreaturesData, and EquipmentData. Let us add the image data library and bit map interface to denzi_-data.h now.

```
// Denzi tiles interface

// Define equipment
#define ITEM_POTION            0 // 1
#define ITEM_WEAPON_SWORD      1 // 2
#define ITEM_ARMOUR_SHEILD     2 // 3
#define ITEM_ARMOUR_LEATHER    3 // 4
#define ITEM_BAG               4
#define ITEM_WEAPON_BOW        5 // 5
#define ITEM_WEAPON_ARROW      6
#define ITEM_MAGIC_BOOTS       7 // 6
#define ITEM_RING              8
#define ITEM_NECKLACE          9
#define ITEM_NOTEBOOK          10
#define ITEM_CANDLE            11
#define ITEM_GAUNTLETS         12
#define ITEM_MUSHROOM          13
#define ITEM_KEY               14
#define ITEM_HELMET            15 // 7
#define ITEM_CHAINMAIL         19 // 8
#define ITEM_BATTLEAXE         25 // 9
#define ITEM_PLATEMAIL         32 // 10
#define ITEM_SPLINTMAIL        33 // 11
#define ITEM_MAGIC_BELT        42 // 12
#define ITEM_MAGIC_SWORD       47 // 13
#define ITEM_POWER_STAFF       48
#define ITEM_FLAMING_SWORD     79 // 14
#define ITEM_LIGHTNING_SWORD 80 // 15
#define ITEM_POWER_SWORD       81 // 16

// Define Creatures
#define CREATURE_SQUID         0
#define CREATURE_BAT           1  // 0
#define CREATURE_SKELETON      2
#define CREATURE_EYE           3
#define CREATURE_ZOMBIE        4
```

```
#define CREATURE_SNAKE        5
#define CREATURE_SNAIL        6
#define CREATURE_DRAGON       7
#define CREATURE_SLIME        8
#define CREATURE_GIANT_BUG    9  // 1
#define CREATURE_REAPER       10
#define CREATURE_CAT          11
#define CREATURE_DOG          12
#define CREATURE_HORSE        13
#define CREATURE_GHOUL        14
#define CREATURE_YETI         15

#define CREATURE_LAND_SQUID   18 // 2
#define CREATURE_MANTICORE    23 // 3
#define CREATURE_SHARK        26 // 4
#define CREATURE_GIANT_RAT    32 // 5
#define CREATURE_GIANT_TICK   36 // 6

#define CREATURE_DRAGON_FLY   70 // 7

// Define terrain
#define TERRAIN_NEW_BRICK     0
#define TERRAIN_USED_BRICK    1
#define TERRAIN_TILE          2
#define TERRAIN_SWIRL         6
#define TERRAIN_CRAGS         8
#define TERRAIN_HILLS         9
#define TERRAIN_GRASSLANDS    10
#define TERRAIN_DIRT_RIGHT    14
#define TERRAIN_DIRT_LEFT     15
#define TERRAIN_WATER         20

#define TERRAIN_MOUNTAINS     90
#define TERRAIN_OAK_FOREST    91
#define TERRAIN_OAK_PRAIRIE   92
#define TERRAIN_PINE_FOREST   93
```

```
#define TERRAIN_PINE_PRAIRIE 94

// Define weather
#define WEATHER_PRECIP_HEAVY 11
#define WEATHER_PRECIP_MEDIUM 12
#define WEATHER_PRECIP_LIGHT 13

// Define structures
#define STRUCTURE_BAR_WINDOW 3
#define STRUCTURE_DOOR_CLOSE 4
#define STRUCTURE_DOOR_OPEN  5
#define STRUCTURE_FOUNTAIN   7
#define STRUCTURE_BIG_TOWER  80
#define STRUCTURE_SMALL_TOWER 81
#define STRUCTURE_KEEP       82
#define STRUCTURE_CASTLE     83
#define STRUCTURE_BIG_CASTLE 84
#define STRUCTURE_TOWER      85
#define STRUCTURE_VILLAGE    86
#define STRUCTURE_TOWN       87
#define STRUCTURE_FARM       88
#define STRUCTURE_MONUMENT   89

// Define characters
#define CHARACTER_BARBARIAN  160
#define CHARACTER_WIZARD     161
#define CHARACTER_RANGER     162
#define CHARACTER_SORCERER   163
#define CHARACTER_CLERIC     164
#define CHARACTER_MONK       164
#define CHARACTER_PALADIN    166
#define CHARACTER_SCOUT      211

extern u8 TerrainCharactersData[], CreaturesData[], EquipmentData[];
```

It is encouraged that everyone create at least one bit map by hand as it is a fun exercise where the creator gets to play the game with their result. The CREATURE_-DRAGON_FLY, TERRAIN_WATER and CHARACTER_SCOUT were created with graph paper by my kids. The hexadecimal values were created by hand and entered into the arrays in place of empty tiles within the original Denzi bit map. I outlined a 16x16 pixel portion of graph paper and asked them to create their picture by putting an X in each graph box they wanted to color. The next step was to convert the X's to 1's and fill in the rest of the 16x16 grid with zero (0)'s. Then split the graph into four rows of bits, each 4 bits (nibble) length. Finally the four bits were converted into nibbles and the resulting hexadecimal value. Here is a picture of the complete worksheet for the dragon fly bit map, including notes for converting binary and hexadecimal. Also see how that the 16x16 boundary was changed on the graph paper to help re-center the image during the creation process.

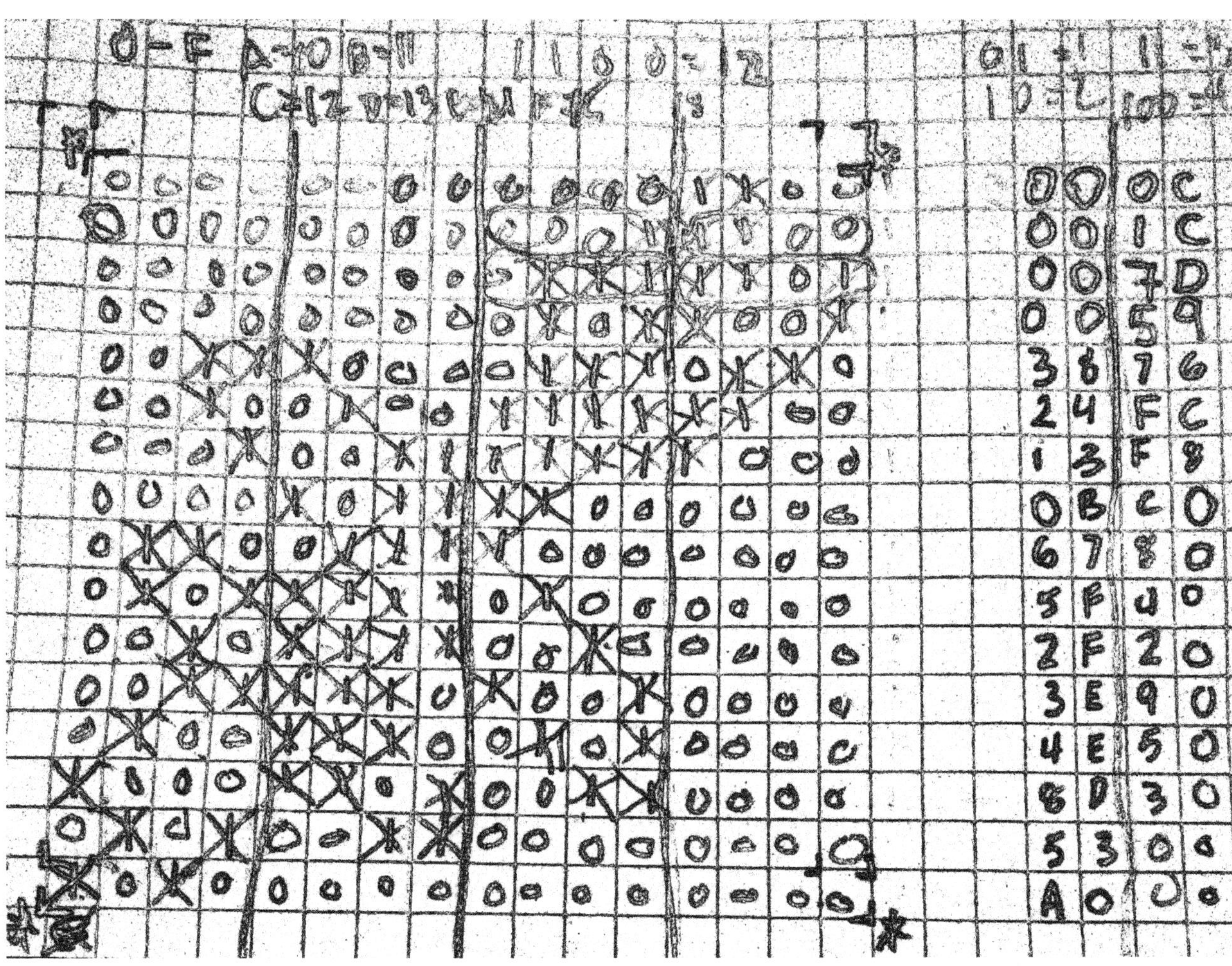

Fig 8: Bitmap worksheet for Dragon Fly

The Denzi binary (black and white) image contains many individual 16x16 pixel images, with 16 of these individual images in each row. Each image is 16 pixels/bits, or two bytes per individual image, or 32 bytes per pixel row for each image. If this example has six (6) rows of 16 images, there would then be 32 bytes per row of pixels, and 6 * 16 or 96 rows of pixels for a total of 3072 bytes of data to represent 96 different binary tiles. To reference, or learn the beginning position of any tile in the array, we can multiply based on the individual image position within the larger image.

Since individual images are 16 rows in height, the next row of images is 572 bytes more (32 bytes for each row and 16 rows) than the last row. Each row of the images must be indexed independently of each other by multiplying the width in pixels (2 * 16) by the row of the tile being read, and then adding the x offset (2 * x) to the resulting index into the bitmap byte array.

```
/*.................................................................*/
/*       width: Return the width in bytes of the tile              */
/*                                                                 */
/*      Return: The tile width in bytes                            */
/*.................................................................*/
#define width() (16 / 8)

/*.................................................................*/
/*      height: Return the height in bytes of the tile             */
/*                                                                 */
/*      Return: The tile height in bytes                           */
/*.................................................................*/
#define height() (16)

/*.................................................................*/
/* total_width: Total width of entire bit map                      */
/*                                                                 */
/*      Return: The tile height in bytes                           */
/*.................................................................*/
#define total_width() (16 * width())

// Global functions
```

```
/*......................................................................*/
/* TilePixel: Return whether or not tile pixle bit is set to one      */
/*                                                                      */
/*      Input: tileSetData the tile set data to reference into         */
/*             tileNum the index into the tile set data                */
/*             x the width positional bit to check                     */
/*             y the height positional bit to check                    */
/*                                                                      */
/*     Return: One (1) if pixel should be illuminated, 0 otherwise     */
/*......................................................................*/
int TilePixel(u8 *tileSetData, int tileNum, u32 x, u32 y)
{
  u32 tilebit;
  int tileY = (tileNum * width()) / total_width();
  int tileX = ((tileNum * width()) & 0x1F) / width();
  u8 *tileColumn = tileSetData +((tileY * height()) +y) *total_width();
  u8 *tileRow = tileColumn + (tileX * width());

  // Ensure x and y inputs are within the valid font size
  if (y >= height())
  {
    return 0;
  }
  if (x >= width() * 8)
  {
    return 0;
  }

  // Shift font bit left based on character width
  // Framebuffer and font map are little endian, so first pixel is low
  // (bit zero or ((1 << 7) >> CHARACTER_WIDTH) and as x increases to
  // higher bits until 7 ((1 << 7) << 0).
  if (x < 8)
  {
    tilebit = ((1 << 7) >> x);
```

```
    // Reference this bit in first byte of tile data. Return if tile
    // bit set or not.
    return ((tileRow[0] & tilebit) ? 1 : 0);
  }
  else
  {
    tilebit = ((1 << 7) >> (x - 8));

    // Reference this bit in second byte of tile data. Return if tile
    // bit set or not.
    return ((tileRow[1] & tilebit) ? 1 : 0);
  }
}
```

Lab 11: Virtual Worlds

11.1 Virtual World Design Overview

The example game we will create in this laboratory book is about a player adventuring within a virtual world. To represent a virtual world, a top down player view is used with pictures that represent portions of the virtual world. With a collection of binary **tiles** that each represent the terrain of a virtual world, the virtual world is constructed with any algorithm of your imagination.

A two dimensional top view of the world can be represented as a **game grid** of base **tiles**, where each **tile** represents a physical portion of the virtual world, with the edge of the screen the boundary of the world. Worlds can be linked to allow the player character to explore much larger worlds.

Individual **game grid tiles** within a game can have stacked or nested **tiles**. For example, the player character walking through the countryside or dungeon. Other **Tiles** stack on top of base Tiles and some can move from one base **Tile** to another. Additional **Tiles**, such as game items, can be added on top of and be picked up off of base **Tiles** by the player. Additionally, a portal can exist on a base **Tile**. The portal can lead to a new **game grid** and virtual world for the player character to explore.

This virtual world will focus on creating compelling random virtual levels that each have a single magical portal that takes the player character to another level within the virtual world, each level with increasing difficulty to the player. This game will be a one way trip that either leads to the demise of the character, or the completion of the game.

11.2 Game Layout

For this world to allow the **tiles** to interact with each other, each **tile** must become more than just a bitmap and color. Software must represent this bitmap as an entity that the player character interacts with. These entities can be classified into three basic types, terrain, creature, and items. Terrain (natural or structures) are base **game grid tiles**, while creatures are **sprites** and items are simply stacked **tiles** as they are displayed on top of the base **tile** but do not move.

The terrain **tiles** of the **game grid** is the physical representation of the virtual world. Terrain, for example, can be grassland, forest, swamp, mountains, desert and water. Structures (townships/buildings) can also be represented as terrain **tiles** within the **game grid**. Creatures include the user controlled player character as well as software controlled creatures of the virtual world. Creatures need hit points, armor class and action characteristics. The interactions between creatures and the character are controlled with software and ultimately determine how fun the game is. Items are any equipment that can be picked up and/or used by the player character. Items for example can be anything worn, wielded or consumed.

The player character **sprite** will move about the **game grid** traveling upon the virtual world of terrain **tiles**. Terrain **tile** flags may indicate whether a or way out, or level up, can be entered through this **tile**. Detailed terrain such as grasslands, rolling hills, mountains, water and crags are defined. Moving up levels is accomplished by finding the magical gate that leads to the way out of the virtual world.

As the player adventures upon the world, various encounters and battles with creatures occur, resulting in a loss of hit points and/or a gain in experience for the player. To communicate the player statistics we use the top left portion of the screen. Let us start by creating a function to display the current character statistics. Name, race, class, attributes and found items all need to be displayed.

```
//
// Game specific Tile flags
//
// Race
#define RACE_HUMAN          (1 << 8)
#define RACE_ELF            (1 << 9)
#define RACE_DWARF          (1 << 10)
#define RACE_HOBIT          (1 << 11)
// Class
#define CLASS_RANGER        (1 << 12)
#define CLASS_SCOUT         (1 << 13)
#define CLASS_WIZARD        (1 << 14)
```

```
#define CLASS_CLERIC          (1 << 15)
//Virtual World
#define IS_PLAYER             (1 << 16)
#define IS_CREATURE           (1 << 17)
#define IS_ITEM               (1 << 18)
#define WORLD_EXIT            (1 << 19)

typedef struct {
  u32 flags;        // Flag bits for behavior, state, etc.
  int hp;           // Health Points
  u8 str, dex, con, intel, wis; // Optional abilities
                                // Can be used with PRNG to determine
                                // if actions are successful
  u8 ac, scratch; // Optional Armour Class and game specific
} SpriteStats;

typedef struct
{
  Tile tile;
  SpriteStats stats;
  World *currentWorld;
  char *name;
} SpriteTile;

typedef struct
{
  SpriteTile player;
  int num_items;
  Tile items[MAX_ITEMS];
} PlayerTile;

// Global variables
PlayerTile TheCharacter;
SpriteTile TheCreatures[MAX_CREATURES];
Tile ExitTile;
extern World TheWorld;
```

```
/*..............................................................*/
/* display_string: display a string on the screen               */
/*                                                               */
/*   Input: string is the string of characters to display        */
/*          x is width pixel position from left                  */
/*          y is height pixel position from top                  */
/*..............................................................*/
void display_string(char *string, int startX, int startY)
{
  for (char *current = string; *current; ++current)
  {
    DisplayCursorChar(*current, startX, startY, COLOR_WHITE);
    startX += 8;
  }
}

/*..............................................................*/
/* player_display: display the players current statistics       */
/*                                                               */
/*   Input: character is pointer to the player                   */
/*..............................................................*/
static void player_display(PlayerTile *character)
{
  int i, len;
  int high, low;

  len = strlen(character->player.name);
  for (i = 0; i < len; ++i)
    DisplayCursorChar(character->player.name[i], i * 8, 10,
                      COLOR_WHITE);

  if (character->player.stats.flags & RACE_HUMAN)
    display_string("Human ", 0, 30);
...
  else if (character->player.stats.flags & CLASS_CLERIC)
```

```
    display_string("Cleric", 48, 30);

  // Strength
  display_string("S:", 0, 50);
  high = (character->player.stats.str >> 4) & 0xF;
  low = character->player.stats.str & 0xF;
  if (high <= 9)
    DisplayCursorChar('0' + high, 16, 50, COLOR_WHITE);
  else
    DisplayCursorChar('A' + high - 10, 16, 50, COLOR_WHITE);
  if (low <= 9)
    DisplayCursorChar('0' + low, 24, 50, COLOR_WHITE);
  else
    DisplayCursorChar('A' + low - 10, 24, 50, COLOR_WHITE);

  // Dexterity
  display_string(" D:", 32, 50);
...
```

11.3 Virtual World Discovery

It is now time to create C language data structures to represent individual **game grid tiles** for terrains, creatures, items and effects. For each of these types we will utilize existing data structures and while introducing PlayerTile, SpriteTile, and SpriteStats structures. This virtual world described is only an example and modeled loosely around typical fantasy roll playing games (RPGs). This foundation could be adopted to any type of virtual world the reader can imagine.

The **game grid** will consist of base **tiles** that represent the virtual world terrain and use the Tile **bit map** index, and color when displaying the **tile**. A flags value is also available to maintain 32 bits of **tile** specific data. The **game grid** uses VISIBLE, REVERSE, FLIP, and INVERSE to affect the orientation and how to display the **bit map**. Other bits are specifically reserved as game specific so please use them. Virtual world flags will be introduced later. These base **tiles** cannot be moved, however, they may be obstructed by **tiles** that are present on top of them, for example, a more complex form of terrain could be water after heavy rainfall, swamp for weeks after and then dessert until the next rain. With Tile's applied on top of Tiles, the virtual terrain can come alive and change dynamically over time.

When the game starts the player does not know where they are so can only see the terrain **tiles** nearby. Let us create a function now that will have the player look around. This should output the type of terrain currently occupied to the console as well as make adjacent base **game grid tiles** visible to the player.

```
// Creature flags
#define VISION                    (1 << 3)
#define TRACKING                  (1 << 4)

...

/*.................................................................*/
/* player_look: Have player examine world, ie current game grid    */
/*                                                                 */
/*    Input: character is pointer to the player                    */
/*.................................................................*/
static void player_look(PlayerTile *character)
{
  World *world = character->player.currentWorld;
  Tile *tiles = world->tiles;
  int x = character->player.locationX,
      y = character->player.locationY;
  const char *terrain;
  int distance, startX, startY, endX, endY, tileNum;

  tileNum = tiles[x + y * GAME_GRID_WIDTH].tileNum;

  // Output the name of the current character occupied terrain
  if (tileNum == TERRAIN_MOUNTAINS)
    terrain = "Mountains";
  else if (tileNum == TERRAIN_OAK_FOREST)
    terrain = "Oak forest";
  else if (tileNum == TERRAIN_OAK_PRAIRIE)
```

```
  terrain = "Oak prairie";
else if (tileNum == TERRAIN_PINE_FOREST)
  terrain = "Pine forest";
else if (tileNum == TERRAIN_PINE_PRAIRIE)
  terrain = "Pine prarie";
else if (tileNum == TERRAIN_CRAGS)
  terrain = "Crags";
else if (tileNum == TERRAIN_HILLS)
  terrain = "Rolling hills";
else if (tileNum == TERRAIN_GRASSLANDS)
  terrain = "Grassland";
else if (tileNum == TERRAIN_WATER)
  terrain = "Water";
else if (tileNum == STRUCTURE_TOWN)
  terrain = "Town";
else
  terrain = "Unknown";
puts(terrain);

// Determine the distance the player can see
if (character->player.stats.flags & TRACKING)
  distance = 5;
else if (character->player.stats.flags & VISION)
  distance = 3;
else
  distance = 1;

startX = x - distance;
if (startX < 0)
  startX = 0;
endX = x + distance;
if (endX >= GAME_GRID_WIDTH)
  endX = GAME_GRID_WIDTH - 1;

startY = y - distance;
if (startY < 0)
```

```
    startY = 0;
  endY = y + distance;
  if (endY >= GAME_GRID_HEIGHT)
    endY = GAME_GRID_HEIGHT - 1;

  // Display all tiles around the character if not already
  for (y = startY; y <= endY; ++y)
  {
    for (x = startX; x <= endX; ++x)
    {
      Tile *theTerrain = GameGridTile(x, y);

      // If not already visible, show tile
      if (!(theTerrain->flags & IS_VISIBLE))
      {
        theTerrain->flags |= IS_VISIBLE;
        TileDisplayGrid(x, y);
      }
    }
  }
}
```

Now, every time the player moves the player_look() function can be called to illuminate more of the game world as the player moves through it.

11.4 Creatures and Items

CreatureTile's must also contain a binary **bitmap** index and color, but the flags may be different. For example, since a creature can move, it must also have a current world location. Also, creatures may carry equipment or items and each have individual creature statistics. To accommodate various creatures, this base CreatureTile will contain statistics as well as primary and secondary **actions**. The CreatureTile structure will use its **bit map** index as a unique identifier to identify different creatures. The statistics of the creature are defined at creation time. Hit points (hp) and armor class (ac) are an integral part of a creatures statistics.

The statistics list for creatures begins with basic statistics, such as strength, dexterity, health or hit points, armor class, experience, etc. This basic structure may also contain another list of abilities, such as tracking (show nearby creatures), attack advantage, and spell casting. Some spells behave similar to an attack, others behave similar to drinking a potion or other use of an item. Each creature **tile** may also represent a group of similar creatures, such as a coordinated group of humans, if that group attacks/defends as a group.

Items are represented as **tiles** that contain a **bit map** index, color, and flags IS_ITEM bit set which indicates the **tile** is item specific. Example items are a potion of healing that would increase the amount of hit points. Another item could have an index indicating a melee weapon. Possession of this item would increase the attack damage of the players primary action if the player type is proficient in such a weapon (class ranger is proficient in swords for example). An item could also modify the characters to hit advantage, to represent and plus one "+1" sword for example.

11.5 Game Randomness

Items and equipment can be dropped by creatures and picked up by the player, creatures can be attacked and/or attack others. In order to create a compelling virtual world there must be some amount of chance or luck within the game to give it life. This randomness is the equivalent of the dice in D&D. Without randomness a virtual world will exhibit a stale static feeling, where every encounter is a mirror of the last. Randomness to the attack attempts. Randomness in the creatures encountered. Randomness in the treasure. Randomness in the world creation itself. With a collection of terrain **tiles** and a creative algorithm, randomly generated worlds can share similar characteristics, but never be the same.

For example a world can be created with coastal flags what will create a world with a coastline as well as give more preference to water or mountain **tiles** if nearby **tiles** are also water or mountains. After checking if a coastline is required, a random terrain **tile** is chosen. In denzi_data.h the following terrain **tiles** will be used; crags, hills, grasslands, water, town as well as mountains, oak forest, oak prarie, pine forest, and pine prarie. To choose we first compute a random value between zero (0) and fifteen (15) and then increase the value to correspond to the intended denzi_data.h index value. The number in comments in denzi_data.h correspond to this zero (0) through fifteen (15) values. This translation from random value to index code is a bit ugly but gets the job done.

```
// Random world flags
#define WORLD_WEST_COAST        (1 << 0)
#define WORLD_EAST_COAST        (1 << 1)
#define WORLD_NORTH_COAST       (1 << 2)
#define WORLD_SOUTH_COAST       (1 << 3)
#define WORLD_MOUNTAINOUS       (1 << 4)

...

/*...........................................................*/
/* world_create_random: Create a game grid of random terrain tiles   */
/*                                                                    */
/*   Input: world is pointer to the game grid                         */
/*          flags indicate world creation preferences                 */
/*                                                                    */
/*  Return: Zero (0)                                                  */
/*...........................................................*/
static int world_create_random(World *world, u32 flags)
{
  Tile *middleEarth = world->tiles;

  int x, y;
  int aboveTile = 0, aboveTileRight = 0, aboveTileLeft = 0;

  // Generate the virtual world
  for (y = 0; y < GAME_GRID_HEIGHT; ++y)
  {
    for (x = 0; x < GAME_GRID_WIDTH; ++x)
    {
      u32 random = rand();
      u32 color = COLOR_GREEN;

      if ((flags & WORLD_NORTH_COAST) && (y == 0))
      {
```

```
    random = TERRAIN_WATER;
    color = COLOR_DEEPSKYBLUE;
}
else if ((flags & WORLD_SOUTH_COAST) &&
         (y >= GAME_GRID_HEIGHT - 2))
{
    random = TERRAIN_WATER;
    color = COLOR_DEEPSKYBLUE;
}
else if ((flags & WORLD_WEST_COAST) && (x == 0))
{
    random = TERRAIN_WATER;
    color = COLOR_DEEPSKYBLUE;
}
else if ((flags & WORLD_EAST_COAST) &&
         (x >= GAME_GRID_WIDTH - 2))
{
    random = TERRAIN_WATER;
    color = COLOR_DEEPSKYBLUE;
}
else
{
  random = (((random & 0xF) ^ ((random & 0xF0) >> 8)) & 0xF) +90;
  if (random > 94)
  {
    if (random == 95)
    {
      random = TERRAIN_CRAGS;
      color = COLOR_SIENNA;
    }
    else if (random == 96)
    {
      random = TERRAIN_HILLS;
      color = COLOR_GOLDEN;
    }
    else if (random == 97)
```

```
    {
      random = TERRAIN_GRASSLANDS;
      color = COLOR_GOLDEN;
    }
    else if (random == 98)
    {
      random = TERRAIN_WATER;
      color = COLOR_DEEPSKYBLUE;
    }
    else if (random == 99)
    {
      random = TERRAIN_WATER;
      color = COLOR_DEEPSKYBLUE;
    }
    else if (random == 100)
    {
      // Make towns very rare
      if ((rand() & 0xF) == 0xF)
      {
        random = STRUCTURE_TOWN;
        color = COLOR_ORANGERED;
      }
      else
      {
        random = TERRAIN_WATER;
        color = COLOR_DEEPSKYBLUE;
      }
    }
    else if (random >= 101)
    {
      random -= 11;
    }
  }

  if (y > 0)
  {
```

```
aboveTile = middleEarth[x + (y - 1) *
                                GAME_GRID_WIDTH].tileNum;
if (x > 0)
  aboveTileLeft = middleEarth[(x - 1) + (y - 1) *
                                GAME_GRID_WIDTH].tileNum;
else
  aboveTileLeft = 0;

if (x < GAME_GRID_WIDTH - 1)
  aboveTileRight = middleEarth[(x + 1) + (y - 1) *
                                GAME_GRID_WIDTH].tileNum;
else
  aboveTileRight = 0;

if (random == TERRAIN_GRASSLANDS)
{
  color = COLOR_GOLDEN;
}

else if ((random != TERRAIN_WATER) &&
       (((flags & (WORLD_WEST_COAST | WORLD_NORTH_COAST)) &&
        (aboveTile == TERRAIN_WATER) &&
           (aboveTileLeft == TERRAIN_WATER)) ||
       ((flags & (WORLD_EAST_COAST | WORLD_SOUTH_COAST)) &&
        (aboveTile == TERRAIN_WATER) &&
           (aboveTileRight == TERRAIN_WATER))))
{
    random = TERRAIN_WATER;
    color = COLOR_DEEPSKYBLUE;
}
else if ((random != TERRAIN_MOUNTAINS) &&
         (flags & WORLD_MOUNTAINOUS) &&
         ((aboveTile == TERRAIN_MOUNTAINS) &&
          (aboveTileLeft == TERRAIN_MOUNTAINS)))
{
  random = TERRAIN_MOUNTAINS;
```

```
          color = COLOR_WHITE;
        }
      }
    }

    // Change color to white if mountains
    if (random == TERRAIN_MOUNTAINS)
      color = COLOR_WHITE;

    // Assign the new terrain tile to the world
    middleEarth[x + y * GAME_GRID_WIDTH].color = color;
    middleEarth[x + y * GAME_GRID_WIDTH].tileNum = random;
    middleEarth[x + y * GAME_GRID_WIDTH].flags = 0;
    middleEarth[x + y * GAME_GRID_WIDTH].list.next = NULL;
    middleEarth[x + y * GAME_GRID_WIDTH].list.previous = NULL;
    middleEarth[x + y * GAME_GRID_WIDTH].bitmap =
                                             TerrainCharactersData;

    // New random number and if bit zero then add reverse flag
    if (rand() & (1 << 0))
      middleEarth[x + y * GAME_GRID_WIDTH].flags = SHOW_REVERSE;

    // If not forest or town, new random to add flipped flag
    if (((middleEarth[x + y * GAME_GRID_WIDTH].tileNum <
          TERRAIN_OAK_FOREST) ||
         (middleEarth[x + y * GAME_GRID_WIDTH].tileNum >
          TERRAIN_PINE_PRAIRIE)) &&
        (middleEarth[x + y * GAME_GRID_WIDTH].tileNum !=
         STRUCTURE_TOWN) && (rand() & (1 << 1)))
      middleEarth[x + y * GAME_GRID_WIDTH].flags = SHOW_FLIPPED;
  }
}

return 0;
}
```

Randomness can also be applied to the creation of the player character. Creating a random player character each game speeds up game play and introduces players to the different types of characters. The following algorithm rolls the player statistics and then chooses a class and race that gives the player the best chance of success in the virtual world.

```
/*.................................................................*/
/* player_create_random: Create a random player character          */
/*                                                                  */
/*    Input: character is pointer to PlayerTile                     */
/*.................................................................*/
static void player_create_random(PlayerTile *character, World *world)
{
  int d6roll;

  bzero(character, sizeof(PlayerTile));

  // Down cast and initialize the sprite
  sprite_initialize((SpriteTile *)character, world);

  // Default adventurer is aggressive with keen vision
  character->player.stats.flags = AGGRESSIVE | VISION;
  character->num_items = 0;

  // Roll 6 sided dice three times for strength
  d6roll = rand() % 6;
  character->player.stats.str = d6roll + 1;
  character->player.stats.str += rand() % 6 + 1; // add another d6
  character->player.stats.str += rand() % 6 + 1; // add another d6

  // Roll 6 sided dice for dexterity
  d6roll = rand() % 6;
  character->player.stats.dex = d6roll + 1;
  character->player.stats.dex += rand() % 6 + 1; // add another d6
  character->player.stats.dex += rand() % 6 + 1; // add another d6
```

```
// Roll 6 sided dice for constitution
d6roll = rand() % 6;
character->player.stats.con = d6roll + 1;
character->player.stats.con += rand() % 6 + 1; // add another d6
character->player.stats.con += rand() % 6 + 1; // add another d6

// Roll 6 sided dice for intelligence
d6roll = rand() % 6;
character->player.stats.intel = d6roll + 1;
character->player.stats.intel += rand() % 6 + 1; // add another d6
character->player.stats.intel += rand() % 6 + 1; // add another d6

// Roll 6 sided dice for wisdom
d6roll = rand() % 6;
character->player.stats.wis = d6roll + 1;
character->player.stats.wis += rand() % 6 + 1; // add another d6
character->player.stats.wis += rand() % 6 + 1; // add another d6

// Determine race/class to optimize abilities

// If intelligence highest, be a wizard
if ((character->player.stats.intel > character->player.stats.dex) &&
    (character->player.stats.intel > character->player.stats.str) &&
    (character->player.stats.intel > character->player.stats.wis))
{
  character->player.stats.flags |= CLASS_WIZARD;
  character->player.stats.hp = 6;
  character->player.tile.color = COLOR_RED;
  character->player.tile.tileNum = CHARACTER_WIZARD;
}

// If wisdom highest, be a cleric
else if ((character->player.stats.wis >
          character->player.stats.dex) &&
         (character->player.stats.wis >
          character->player.stats.intel) &&
```

```
        (character->player.stats.wis > character->player.stats.str))
{
  character->player.stats.flags |= CLASS_CLERIC;
  character->player.stats.hp = 8;
  character->player.tile.color = COLOR_RED;
  character->player.tile.tileNum = CHARACTER_CLERIC;
}

// If dexterity highest, be a scout
else if ((character->player.stats.dex >
          character->player.stats.wis) &&
         (character->player.stats.dex >
          character->player.stats.intel) &&
         (character->player.stats.dex > character->player.stats.str))
{
  character->player.stats.flags |= CLASS_SCOUT | TRACKING;
  character->player.stats.hp = 8;
  character->player.tile.color = COLOR_RED;
  character->player.tile.tileNum = CHARACTER_SCOUT;
}

// Otherwise be a ranger
else
{
  character->player.stats.flags |= CLASS_RANGER | TRACKING;
  character->player.tile.color = COLOR_RED;
  character->player.tile.tileNum = CHARACTER_BARBARIAN;
  character->player.stats.hp = 10;
}

// If high constitution, be human
if (character->player.stats.con > 10)
{
  character->player.stats.flags |= RACE_HUMAN;
  character->player.stats.str += 1;
  character->player.stats.dex += 1;
```

```
    character->player.stats.con += 1;
    character->player.stats.intel += 1;
    character->player.stats.wis += 1;
  }

  // Otherwise optimize for class
  else if (character->player.stats.flags & CLASS_RANGER)
  {
    character->player.stats.flags |= RACE_DWARF;
    character->player.stats.str += 2;
    character->player.stats.con += 2;
  }

  else if (character->player.stats.flags & CLASS_WIZARD)
  {
    character->player.stats.flags |= RACE_ELF;
    character->player.stats.intel += 1;
    character->player.stats.dex += 2;
  }
  else if (character->player.stats.flags & CLASS_CLERIC)
  {
    character->player.stats.flags |= RACE_DWARF;
    character->player.stats.wis += 1;
    character->player.stats.con += 2;
  }
  else if (character->player.stats.flags & CLASS_SCOUT)
  {
    character->player.stats.flags |= RACE_HOBIT;
    character->player.stats.dex += 2;
    character->player.stats.con += 1;
  }
  else
    puts("FATAL ERROR!");

  // Compute the AC based on no armor and dexterity modifier
  character->player.stats.ac = 10;
```

```
  if (character->player.stats.dex > 10)
    character->player.stats.ac +=
       ((character->player.stats.dex - 10) >> 1); // (Dex - 10) / 2

  // Configure for 1st level, no experience
  character->player.currentWorld->level = 1;
  character->player.currentWorld->score = 0;

  character->player.name = "xlawless";
  character->player.name[0] = rand() % 32 + 'A';

  character->player.tile.bitmap = TerrainCharactersData;
  character->player.tile.flags = IS_PLAYER | IS_VISIBLE|NO_FLIP;
}
```

Now let us put it all together and create our random virtual world game. The random world will have a randomly generated player character located in a random location within a randomly generated virtual world that is a **game grid** of terrain **tiles**. Also existing within this virtual world are randomly chosen creatures in random locations within the **game grid**. The goal of the game is to find the gate to the next level while battling or avoiding the creatures who, when defeated, may drop items of value for the player to gather and use.

When the game starts there are two types of creatures, giant beetles and bats. Eventually giant beetles pursue the player while bats fly away. Giant beetles are also stronger and have more hit points. As the player progresses to higher levels, more creatures are introduced. The land squid and white shark hide and ambush the player while the manticore and dragon fly with long range attacks that make defeating them an increasing challenge. For now these creatures do nothing but appear on the screen but in one more chapter they will take on a life of their own.

```
/*...........................................................*/
/* game_start: Start the virtual world                       */
/*                                                           */
/*   Input: character is pointer to PlayerTile               */
/*          creatures is pointer to array of CreatureTile's  */
/*          world is pointer to game grid of TerrainTile's   */
/*          period is number of micro seconds between game rounds   */
/*...........................................................*/
static void game_start(PlayerTile *character, SpriteTile *creatures,
                World *world, int gamePeriod)
{
  int i, randX, randY, locationFound;
  BackgroundTile *middleEarth = world->tiles;
  u32 divisor = (GAME_GRID_WIDTH - 1) | 0xF;

  for (i = 0; i < character->level + 1; ++i)
  {
    if (i < 8)
    {
      int roll = rand();

      if ((roll % 100) < 50)
      {
        creatures[i].tile.color = COLOR_BROWN;
        creatures[i].tile.flags = IS_VISIBLE | IS_CREATURE | NO_FLIP;
        creatures[i].tile.tileNum = CREATURE_GIANT_BUG;
        creatures[i].stats.ac = 15;
        creatures[i].stats.hp = 9 + i;
        creatures[i].stats.str = 16;
        creatures[i].stats.dex = 12;
        creatures[i].stats.intel = 4;
        creatures[i].stats.con = 10;
        creatures[i].stats.wis = 3;
        creatures[i].stats.flags = AGGRESSIVE | VISION | TRACKING;
        creatures[i].name = "Giant Beetle";
      }
```

```
      else
      {
...
      }
    }
    else if (i < 16)
    {
      int roll = rand();

      if ((roll % 100) < 50)
      {
        creatures[i].tile.color = COLOR_ORANGERED;
        creatures[i].tile.flags = IS_CREATURE | NO_FLIP;
        creatures[i].tile.tileNum = CREATURE_LAND_SQUID;
...
      }
      else
      {
...
      }
    }
    else
    {
      int roll = rand();

      if ((roll % 100) < 45)
      {
        creatures[i].tile.color = COLOR_GOLDEN;
        creatures[i].tile.flags = IS_VISIBLE | IS_CREATURE |
                                  NO_FLIP;
        creatures[i].tile.tileNum = CREATURE_MANTICORE;
        creatures[i].stats.ac = 20;
        creatures[i].stats.hp = i;
        creatures[i].stats.str = 16;
        creatures[i].stats.dex = 16;
        creatures[i].stats.intel = 4;
```

```
        creatures[i].stats.con = 10;
        creatures[i].stats.wis = 3;
        creatures[i].stats.flags = AGGRESSIVE | FLYING | VISION|AMBUSH;
        creatures[i].name = "Manticore";
      }
      else if ((roll % 100) < 90)
      {
...
      }
      else
      {
        creatures[i].tile.color = COLOR_YELLOW;
        creatures[i].tile.flags = IS_VISIBLE | IS_CREATURE;
        creatures[i].tile.tileNum = CREATURE_DRAGON_FLY;
        creatures[i].stats.ac = 24;
        creatures[i].stats.hp = 25 + i;
        creatures[i].stats.str = 18;
        creatures[i].stats.dex = 18;
        creatures[i].stats.intel = 10;
        creatures[i].stats.con = 18;
        creatures[i].stats.wis = 13;
        creatures[i].stats.flags = AGGRESSIVE | FLYING | VISION |
                                   TRACKING;
        creatures[i].name = "Dragon Wasp";
      }
    }
```

After generating the random creature a random starting location is calculated. The random location is repeated until a location is found that is compatible with the creature. Flying creatures can be anywhere, land squids cannot be in mountains, sharks can only be in water and giant beetles cannot be in water.

```
// Loop to find a random starting place on the game grid
for (;;)
{
  randX = rand() & divisor;
  if (randX > GAME_GRID_WIDTH - 1)
    randX -= 5;
  randY = rand() & divisor;
  if (randY > GAME_GRID_HEIGHT - 1)
    randY -= 5;

  // Flying creatures can spawn anywhere so break
  if (creatures[i].stats.flags & FLYING)
    break;

  // Check if creature can be in the mountains
  if (middleEarth[randX + randY * GAME_GRID_WIDTH].tileNum ==
                                              TERRAIN_MOUNTAINS)
  {
    if (creatures[i].tile.tileNum == CREATURE_LAND_SQUID)
      continue;
  }

  if (middleEarth[randX + randY * GAME_GRID_WIDTH].
                                   tileNum == TERRAIN_WATER)
  {
    // Sharks can only be in water
    if (creatures[i].tile.tileNum == CREATURE_SHARK)
      break;

    if (creatures[i].tile.tileNum == CREATURE_GIANT_BUG)
      continue;
  }
  else if (creatures[i].tile.tileNum == CREATURE_SHARK)
    continue;

  // Otherwise this location is great so start creature here
```

```
      break;
    }

    // Initialize the creature sprite and append it to the game grid
    creatures[i].locationX = randX;
    creatures[i].locationY = randY;
    ListAppend(&creatures[i], GameGridTile(randX, randY));
  }
```

Finally, spawn the player character in a random location. Then display the character stats and have the player look around at the nearby terrain **tiles**.

```
  // Display the character in a random location
  locationFound = 0;
  while (!locationFound)
  {
    randX = rand() & divisor;//0x2F;
    if (randX > GAME_GRID_WIDTH - 1) // Needed for 28 (640x480)
      randX -= 5;
    randY = rand() & divisor;
    if (randY > GAME_GRID_HEIGHT - 1)
      randY -= 5;
    if ((middleEarth[randX + randY * GAME_GRID_WIDTH].
                                tile.tileNum == TERRAIN_MOUNTAINS) ||
        (middleEarth[randX + randY * GAME_GRID_WIDTH].
                                     tile.tileNum == TERRAIN_WATER))
      locationFound = 0;
    else
      locationFound = 1;
  }

  character->player.currentWorld = world;
  character->player.locationX = randX;
  character->player.locationY = randY;
  middleEarth[randX + randY * GAME_GRID_WIDTH].sprite =
                                                     &character->player;
```

```
  // Look around
  player_look(character);

  // Display the character details on top left of screen
  player_display(character);
}
```

To start the game we put together the pieces created so far. After clearing the screen and seeding the random number generator, we create a random player and random world before starting the game, which spawns the creatures and player upon the new world.

```
/*...................................................................*/
/* GameStart: Shell interface command to start the game              */
/*                                                                   */
/*    Input: command is an unused parameter                          */
/*                                                                   */
/*   Return: TASK_FINISHED                                           */
/*...................................................................*/
int GameStart(const char *command)
{
  if (ScreenUp)
  {
    // Clear the screen first
    ScreenClear();

    // Seed the PRNG
    srand(TimerNow() ^ 'G');

    TheWorld.tiles = (void *)MiddleEarth;
    TheWorld.x = GAME_GRID_WIDTH;
    TheWorld.y = GAME_GRID_HEIGHT;

    player_create_random(&TheCharacter);

    world_create_random(&TheWorld, 0);
```

```
    game_start(&TheCharacter, TheCreatures, &TheWorld,
               MICROS_PER_SECOND);

    GameUp = TRUE;
    ConsoleState.puts("\nAdventure awaits!");

  }
  else
    puts("Video screen not initialized");

  return TASK_FINISHED;
}
```

11.6 Player Movement

The code to move the player does three things. First it checks if the move is valid and the new base **tile** terrain is allowed for the player. Mountains are impassible without magic boots and water is impassible without the belt of swimming. The second step is to remove the player SpriteTile from the current base **tile** list and redraw the **game grid tile** with TileDisplayGrid(). The third and final step is to append the SpriteTile to the destination base **game grid Tile** and redraw it.

```
/*...................................................................*/
/* player_move: Move the player sprite to a new game grid location   */
/*                                                                   */
/*   Input: characterTile is pointer to PlayerTile                   */
/*          tileX is the players new tile X position                 */
/*          tileY is the players new tile Y position                 */
/*                                                                   */
/*  Return: Zero (0) on success, -1 on failure                       */
/*...................................................................*/
static int player_move(PlayerTile *characterTile, int tileX, int tileY)
{
  Tile *theTerrain = GameGridTile(tileX, tileY);
```

```
if (theTerrain->tileNum == TERRAIN_MOUNTAINS)
{
  int i;

  for (i = 0; i < characterTile->num_items; ++i)
    if (characterTile->items[i].tileNum == ITEM_MAGIC_BOOTS)
      break;

  if (!i || (i == characterTile->num_items))
  {
    puts("Mountains impassible");
    return -1;
  }
}
if (theTerrain->tileNum == TERRAIN_WATER)
{
  int i;

  for (i = 0; i < characterTile->num_items; ++i)
    if (characterTile->items[i].tileNum == ITEM_MAGIC_BELT)
      break;

  if (!i || (i == characterTile->num_items))
  {
    puts("Water impassible");
    return -1;
  }
  else
    puts("Belt of Swimming");
}

// Move player sprite to the new game grid location if valid
if (theTerrain)
{
  // Remove the sprite from the previous game grid tile
  ListRemove(characterTile->player.tile.list);
```

```
    TileDisplayGrid(characterTile->player.locationX,
                    characterTile->player.locationY);

    // Append the player to the new terrain base tile
    characterTile->player.locationX = tileX;
    characterTile->player.locationY = tileY;
    ListAppend(characterTile, theTerrain);

    // Display new location and look around
    TileDisplayGrid(tileX, tileY);
    player_look(characterTile);

    // If this is a world exit, level up
    if (theTerrain->flags & WORLD_EXIT)
      game_level_up(characterTile);
  }
  else
    puts("player destination not found, player lost!");
  return 0;
}
```

11.7 Experience and Levels

Two core concepts of the virtual world are going through the gate to level up, and gaining experience within the virtual world. Leveling up introduces more powerful creatures as well as more difficult terrain. A level up will generate a new random **game grid** of terrain **tiles**, with additional flags that increase the amount of water and/or mountain terrain to make it more difficult for the player. Gaining experience is achieved with every creature defeated and gives the player additional advantage on attacks as well as damage once enough experience is accumulated.

Let us first create code for going through the game and up a game level. On level up, wizards have time to apply the experience they have obtained, so check if a wizards attack bonus increases because of their experience. Then create a new random world of increasing difficulty by adding additional flags to the world creation. Leveling up essentially starts a new game with the same player character so finally start the newly created game to complete the level up.

```
/*...............................................................*/
/* game_level_up: Transition game to new level                   */
/*                                                               */
/*   Input: characterTile is void pointer to PlayerTile          */
/*...............................................................*/
static void game_level_up(PlayerTile *characterTile)
{
  World *world = characterTile->player.currentWorld;
  int num_creatures;

  // Clear the screen first
  ScreenClear();

  // Reseed the PRNG
  srand(TimerNow() ^ ('L' +characterTile->player.currentWorld->score));

  // The portal advances levels
  if (characterTile->player.currentWorld->level < MAX_CREATURES - 1)
    ++characterTile->player.currentWorld->level;

  num_creatures = characterTile->player.currentWorld->level + 1;

  // Increase creatures per level depending on game grid size
  if (num_creatures > GAME_GRID_WIDTH)
    world_create_random(world, WORLD_WEST_COAST | WORLD_NORTH_COAST |
             WORLD_EAST_COAST | WORLD_SOUTH_COAST | WORLD_MOUNTAINOUS);
  else if (num_creatures > GAME_GRID_WIDTH -
          (GAME_GRID_WIDTH / 4))
    world_create_random(world, WORLD_NORTH_COAST | WORLD_WEST_COAST |
                        WORLD_MOUNTAINOUS);
  else if (num_creatures > GAME_GRID_WIDTH / 2)
    world_create_random(world, WORLD_NORTH_COAST | WORLD_WEST_COAST);
  else if (num_creatures > GAME_GRID_WIDTH / 8)
```

```
    world_create_random(world, WORLD_NORTH_COAST);
  else
    world_create_random(world, 0);

  // Start the virtual world game
  game_start(characterTile, TheCreatures, world);
}
```

Let us add a step at game_start() to add an exit gate tile to the **game grid**. This exit gate tile is placed in a random location on the **game grid** that is not a water or mountain terrain. If the player character enters the base **tile** that contains this gate tile it will call the game_level_up() function to move the player to a new virtual world.

```
  // Display the teleportation gate in a random location
  locationFound = 0;
  while (!locationFound)
  {
    randX = rand() & divisor;
    if (randX > GAME_GRID_WIDTH - 1)
      randX -= 5;
    randY = rand() & divisor;
    if (randY > GAME_GRID_HEIGHT - 1)
      randY -= 5;

    // Do not allow the gate location to be in mountains or water
    if ((middleEarth[randX + randY * GAME_GRID_WIDTH].tileNum ==
         TERRAIN_MOUNTAINS) || (middleEarth[randX + randY *
                        GAME_GRID_WIDTH].tileNum == TERRAIN_WATER))
      locationFound = 0;

    // Do not let the portal location be the edge
    else if (!randX || !randY ||
             (randX == GAME_GRID_WIDTH - 1) ||
             (randY == GAME_GRID_HEIGHT - 1))
      locationFound = 0;
    else
```

```
        locationFound = 1;
    }

    // Mark terrain tile as the world exit
    ExitTile.bitmap = TerrainCharactersData;
    ExitTile.color = COLOR_MAGENTA;
    ExitTile.flags = IS_VISIBLE;
    ExitTile.list.next = NULL;
    ExitTile.list.previous = NULL;
    ExitTile.tileNum = STRUCTURE_DOOR_OPEN;
    middleEarth[randX + randY * GAME_GRID_WIDTH].flags |= WORLD_EXIT;
    ListAppend(&ExitTile, &middleEarth[randX + randY * GAME_GRID_WIDTH]);
```

Congratulations, now we have a Virtual World the player can explore, each level getting more difficult to navigate. This leads us directly into the final chapter where we breath life into this Virtual World and solidify our understanding of system software and the C language.

Chapter 12: Players and Creatures

12.0 Learning Through Code Review

While previous chapters have also done this, this chapter is focused on reading and understanding the virtual_world.c source code for the adventure game. Each section introduces the next portion of source code to be reviewed, explains its purpose and then displays the source code. It is important for the reader to read and understand the source code, especially relating the comments to the code below those comments. If parts of the C source code does not make sense the reader should review chapter 3 of the main book, or 4 if the confusion is pointer related. If anything is still confusing the reader is encouraged to research their questions on the Internet. If the readers confusion is resolved by their own research of outside sources, please report the confusion to the author so it can hopefully be addressed in the next version of the book.

12.1 Creature Movement

Creatures are sprites and they move the same as the player sprite. However, some creatures can fly or otherwise traverse terrain tiles that the player cannot, so separate but very similar sprite_move() and sprite_move_callback() functions need to be created. One difference between the player and the creature movements are that the creatures can only move one tile per game period so the effect period is increased so the movement appears smoother as one round blends into the next. This also gives the player the advantage in that they can always outrun a creature.

```
/*...............................................................*/
/* sprite_move_callback: Timer callback for sprite move effect      */
/*                                                                  */
/*   Input: id is unused                                            */
/*          data is the ActionTile pointer                          */
/*          context is the game grid Tile pointer                   */
/*                                                                  */
/*  Return: TASK_FINISHED                                           */
/*...............................................................*/
int sprite_move_callback(u32 id, void *data, void *context)
{
  SpriteTile *spriteTile = data;

  StdioState = &ConsoleState;

  // If effect active perform the next effect and update count
  if (spriteTile->effect.count)
    TileEffectNext((EffectTile *)spriteTile);

  // If effect still active, schedule the next effect
  if (spriteTile->effect.count)
  {
    TimerSchedule(spriteTile->effect.period,
                  sprite_move_callback, spriteTile, context);
  }
  else
  {
    Tile *currentTile;

    // Remove the sprite from the previous game grid tile
    ListRemove(spriteTile->effect.tile.list);

    // Append sprite to the end of the new tile list
    currentTile = GameGridTile(spriteTile->effect.locationX,
                               spriteTile->effect.locationY);
    if (currentTile)
```

```
      ListAppend(spriteTile,currentTile);
    else
      puts("sprite destination not found, sprite lost!");
  }

  return TASK_FINISHED;
}

/*...................................................................*/
/* sprite_move: Move sprite to a new background tile                */
/*                                                                   */
/*   Input: creatureTile is pointer to creature sprite to move      */
/*          tileX indicate the new X tile position                  */
/*          tileY indicate the new Y tile position                  */
/*                                                                   */
/*  Return: Zero (0) on success, -1 if error                        */
/*...................................................................*/
static int sprite_move(SpriteTile *creatureTile, int tileX, int tileY)
{

  // Silent return if effect is already in progress
  if ((creatureTile->effect.locationX !=
      creatureTile->effect.destinationX) ||
      (creatureTile->effect.count))
    return -1;

  // Flying creatures can go anywhere, so only check non-flyers
  if (!(creatureTile->stats.flags & FLYING))
  {
    Tile *newTile = GameGridTile(tileX, tileY);

    if (newTile == NULL)
      return -1;

    // Land squids can't go in the mountains
    if (newTile->tileNum == TERRAIN_MOUNTAINS)
```

```
    {
      if (creatureTile->effect.tile.tileNum == CREATURE_LAND_SQUID)
        return -1;
    }

    // Giant bugs cannot swim
    if (newTile->tileNum == TERRAIN_WATER)
    {
      if (creatureTile->effect.tile.tileNum == CREATURE_GIANT_BUG)
        return -1;
    }

    // And sharks cannot leave the water
    else if (creatureTile->effect.tile.tileNum == CREATURE_SHARK)
        return -1;

  }

  // Hide creature and redraw original tile
  creatureTile->effect.tile.flags &= ~IS_VISIBLE;
  TileDisplayGrid(creatureTile->effect.locationX,
                  creatureTile->effect.locationY);

  // Make moving creatures visible
  creatureTile->effect.tile.flags |= IS_VISIBLE;

  // Configure sprite movement effect
  // Total time of effect is effect.total * effect.period

  // Initialize the move effect
  creatureTile->effect.total = 4; // 1 or power of 2
  creatureTile->effect.period = MICROS_PER_SECOND / 4;

  // Assign the effect callback function invoked every period
  creatureTile->effect.poll = sprite_move_callback;
```

```
  // Start the move player effect tile
  return TileEffectStart(&creatureTile->effect, tileX, tileY);
}
```

12.2 Player and Creature Actions

This virtual world is a world filled with monsters, magic and medieval weaponry so the game **actions** are attacks, either short range or long range. A ranged weapon type can attack a creature from a distance (multiple game grid tiles away). The same algorithm can be used for spells such as magic missile. It is only possible to attack creatures that have been detected and are within range. Let us create an attack_range() function now that determines the best attack type between two sprites based on the distance between them. Short range, or melee, attacks are preferred over ranged attacks. This function also takes into account whether the attacker or target are on a terrain base tile that prevents an attack.

Read through the code below to see how the attack_range() function is organized and written.

```
/*...................................................................*/
/* attack_range: Determine range and return action that can reach    */
/*                                                                   */
/*   Input: creatureTile is the attacking creature                   */
/*          nearbyCreatureTile is the creature being attacked        */
/*                                                                   */
/*  Return: Pointer to ActionTile that can reach or NULL             */
/*...................................................................*/
static ActionTile *attack_range(SpriteTile *creatureTile,
                                SpriteTile *nearbyCreatureTile)
{
  Tile *creatureTerrain = GameGridTile(creatureTile->effect.locationX,
                                       creatureTile->effect.locationY);
  Tile *nearbyCreatureTerrain = GameGridTile(
                                 nearbyCreatureTile->effect.locationX,
                                 nearbyCreatureTile->effect.locationY);
```

```
int deltaX, deltaY;

if (creatureTile->effect.locationX >
    nearbyCreatureTile->effect.locationX)
  deltaX = creatureTile->effect.locationX -
           nearbyCreatureTile->effect.locationX;
else
  deltaX = nearbyCreatureTile->effect.locationX -
           creatureTile->effect.locationX;

if (creatureTile->effect.locationY >
    nearbyCreatureTile->effect.locationY)
  deltaY = creatureTile->effect.locationY -
           nearbyCreatureTile->effect.locationY;
else
  deltaY = nearbyCreatureTile->effect.locationY -
           creatureTile->effect.locationY;

// If more that one space away then check ranged attacks
if ((deltaX > 1) || (deltaY > 1))
{
  // If a ranged weapon is present
  if (creatureTile->stats.second.affect > 0)
  {
    if (!(creatureTile->stats.flags & FLYING))
    {
      // Ensure player is not trying to attack from the water
      if (creatureTerrain->tileNum == TERRAIN_WATER)
      {
        if (creatureTile->effect.tile.flags & IS_PLAYER)
          puts("Cannot fire while Swimming");
        return NULL;
      }

      // Ensure player is not trying to attack into the mountains
      if (nearbyCreatureTerrain->tileNum == TERRAIN_MOUNTAINS)
```

```
        {
          if (creatureTile == &TheCharacter.player)
            puts("Mountains hide opponent");
          return NULL;
        }
      }

      // Return no attack if out of range
      if ((deltaX > creatureTile->stats.second.range) ||
          (deltaY > creatureTile->stats.second.range))
        return NULL;

      // Otherwise return ranged attack
      return &creatureTile->stats.second;
    }
    return NULL;
  }

  // Otherwise prefer melee (primary) attack
  else if (creatureTile->stats.first.affect > 0)
  {
    // If this is the character ensure this is a valid attack
    if (creatureTile == &TheCharacter.player)
    {
      // Check to ensure player is not trying to attack from the water
      PlayerTile *characterTile = &TheCharacter;

      if (creatureTerrain->tileNum == TERRAIN_WATER)
      {
        puts("Cannot attack while Swimming");
        return NULL;
      }

      // Ensure player is not trying to attack into the mountains
      if (nearbyCreatureTerrain->tileNum == TERRAIN_MOUNTAINS)
      {
```

```
        int i;

        for (i = 0; i < characterTile->num_items; ++i)
          if (characterTile->items[i].tileNum == ITEM_MAGIC_BOOTS)
            break;

        if (!i || (i == characterTile->num_items))
        {
          if (creatureTile->stats.second.affect)
            return &creatureTile->stats.second;
          else
          {
            puts("Mountains out of reach");
            return NULL;
          }
        }
      }
    }

    // Return the default short range melee weapon
    return &creatureTile->stats.first;
  }

  // Otherwise return to attack within range
  else
    return NULL;
}
```

Finally, the creature_attack() function is created. This function takes the ActionTile returned from attack_range() and rolls the dice to see if the attack succeeds. When the player or creature attacks from a hidden position they get a surprise attack bonus and then immediately become visible. Ranged attacks add the dexterity modifier and melee attacks add the attacking creatures strength modifier. Player stats and class may also change the attack modifier.

```
/*..................................................................*/
/* creature_attack: One creature attacks another                    */
/*                                                                  */
/*   Input: creatureTile is pointer to attacking creature/sprite    */
/*          attack the type of attack action                        */
/*          attackedCreatureTile is the creature being attacked     */
/*..................................................................*/
static void creature_attack(SpriteTile *creatureTile,
                            ActionTile *attackTile,
                            SpriteTile *attackedCreatureTile)
{
  // Roll virtual dice (sample PRNG)
  int d20roll, modifier = 0;

  // Silent return if attack effect is already in progress
  if (attackTile->effect.count)
    return;

  // Simulate 20 side dice roll with 8 bits worth or randomness
  d20roll = (rand() % 31);
  if (d20roll == 0)
    d20roll = 20;

  // If overflow, trim the value
  if (d20roll > 20)
    d20roll -= d20roll - 20;

  // If an ambush, give advantage to the roll
  if (!(creatureTile->effect.tile.flags & IS_VISIBLE))
  {
    int roll;

    roll = (rand() % 31);
    if (roll == 0)
      roll = 20;
    if (roll > 20)
```

```
      roll -= roll - 20;

    // Use second roll if higher
    if (roll > d20roll)
      d20roll = roll;
  }

  // Apply dexterity modifier if ranged attack
  if (attackTile->range > 1)
  {
    if (creatureTile->stats.dex > 10)
      modifier = (creatureTile->stats.dex - 10) >> 1;
  }

  // Otherwise apply strength modifier
  else if (creatureTile->stats.str > 10)
    modifier = (creatureTile->stats.str - 10) >> 1;

  // If character, apply proficiency modifier
  //   2 plus one every four levels
  if (creatureTile == &TheCharacter.player)
  {
    // Apply more class/race specific additions here
    if ((TheCharacter.player.stats.flags & CLASS_WIZARD) &&
        (creatureTile->stats.intel > 10))
      modifier = 2 + (TheCharacter.player.currentWorld->score >> 3) +
                 ((creatureTile->stats.intel - 10) >> 1);

    else if (TheCharacter.player.stats.flags & CLASS_RANGER)
      modifier += 2 + (TheCharacter.player.currentWorld->score >> 3);

    // Cleric has no base proficiency but experience
    else if (TheCharacter.player.stats.flags & CLASS_CLERIC)
      modifier += (TheCharacter.player.currentWorld->score >> 3);

    // Scout has proficiency and uses dexterity for proficiency
```

```
    else if (TheCharacter.player.stats.flags & CLASS_SCOUT)
    {
      if (creatureTile->stats.dex > 10)
        modifier = 2 + (TheCharacter.player.currentWorld->score >> 3) +
                 ((creatureTile->stats.dex - 10) >> 1);
      else
        modifier = 2 + (TheCharacter.player.currentWorld->score >> 3);
    }
  }

  // If character involved, display creature name at start of attack
  if ((creatureTile == &TheCharacter.player) ||
      (attackedCreatureTile == &TheCharacter.player))
    puts(creatureTile->name);
...

  // Set the color of the action tile to hit (red) or miss (blue)
  if (d20roll + modifier >= attackedCreatureTile->stats.ac)
    attackTile->effect.tile.color = COLOR_RED;
  else
    attackTile->effect.tile.color = COLOR_BLUE;

  // Initialize the move effect
  attackTile->effect.total = 4; // 1 or power of 2
  attackTile->effect.period = MICROS_PER_SECOND / 16;
  attackTile->effect.locationX = creatureTile->effect.locationX;
  attackTile->effect.locationY = creatureTile->effect.locationY;

  // Assign the effect callback function invoked every period
  attackTile->effect.poll = attack_callback;
  attackTile->effect.tile.list.next = NULL;

  // Add creature as previous tile that launched effect
  attackTile->effect.tile.list.previous = (void *)creatureTile;

  // Start the move player effect tile
```

```
  TileEffectStart((EffectTile *)attackTile,
                  attackedCreatureTile->effect.locationX,
                  attackedCreatureTile->effect.locationY);

  // Make attacking sprites visible
  creatureTile->effect.tile.flags |= IS_VISIBLE;
}
```

It is also necessary to define the effect callback function attack_callback() to handle displaying each visual effect of the attack. The actual bitmap displayed for the attack effect depends on the creature or player weapon currently in use.

```
/*...................................................................*/
/* attack_callback: Timer invoked callback for attack effect         */
/*                                                                   */
/*   Input: id is unused                                             */
/*          data is the ActionTile pointer                           */
/*          context is the game grid Tile pointer                    */
/*                                                                   */
/*  Return: Zero (0) on success, -1 if error                         */
/*...................................................................*/
int attack_callback(u32 id, void *data, void *context)
{
  ActionTile *actionTile = data;

  StdioState = &ConsoleState;

  // If effect active perform the next effect and update count
  if (actionTile->effect.count)
    TileEffectNext((EffectTile *)actionTile);

  // If effect still active, schedule the next effect
  if (actionTile->effect.count)
  {
    TimerSchedule(actionTile->effect.period,
                  attack_callback, actionTile, context);
```

```
    return TASK_FINISHED;
  }

  // If destination is visible, redraw it without attack effect
  TileDisplayGrid(actionTile->effect.destinationX,
                  actionTile->effect.destinationY);

  return TASK_FINISHED;
}
```

12.3 Damage and Defeated Creatures

It is important to perform a random attack roll, add attack bonus and compare with the armor class of the creature being attacked to see if the attack was successful. If the attack is success take damage from the other creature and if the creature hit points goes below zero it is defeated so we remove it from the game grid. If the player defeated the creature we give the player an experience point and roll to see if the defeated creature dropped an item. As the player increases in level, more powerful items are dropped. This code is added to creature_attack() after the TileEffectStart() call.

```
...
  // Compare the modified roll to the attackedCreatureTile armour class
  if (d20roll + modifier >= attackedCreatureTile->stats.ac)
  {
    int i, damage;

    // Loop for each d6 roll for the attack
    for (i = 0, damage = 0; i < attackTile->affect; ++i)
      damage += (rand() % 6) + 1;

    // If an ambush, double the damage
    if (!(creatureTile->effect.tile.flags & IS_VISIBLE))
    {
      for (i = 0; i < attackTile->affect; ++i)
        damage += (rand() % 6) + 1;
```

```
    putbyte(damage);

    // Add the visible flag as it is one time use
    creatureTile->effect.tile.flags |= IS_VISIBLE;
  }

  // Apply attack bonus for creatureTile to the virtual roll
  attackedCreatureTile->stats.hp -= damage + modifier;

  // If character involved, display damage from attack
  if ((creatureTile == &TheCharacter.player) ||
      (attackedCreatureTile == &TheCharacter.player))
  {
    putbyte(damage + modifier);
    puts(" damage!");
  }

  // Check if attacked creature dies
  if (attackedCreatureTile->stats.hp < 0)
  {
    int x = attackedCreatureTile->effect.locationX,
        y = attackedCreatureTile->effect.locationY;

    // Unlink this creature from the game grid tile
    ListRemove(attackedCreatureTile->effect.tile.list);

    // Flag creature as dead
    attackedCreatureTile->effect.tile.flags |= IS_DEAD;

    // Display the terrain again
    TileDisplayGrid(x, y);

    // If the attacking creature is the character
    if (creatureTile->effect.tile.flags & IS_PLAYER)
    {
```

```
        if (creatureTile != &TheCharacter.player)
          puts("ERROR: Creature is not player but has flag set!");

        // Update character and check if creature dropped anything
        defeat_creature(&TheCharacter, attackedCreatureTile);
      }
    }

    // If the attacked creature is the character, update HP
    if (attackedCreatureTile->effect.tile.flags & IS_PLAYER)
      player_display(&TheCharacter);
  }
  else
  {
    // If character involved, display attack missed
    if ((creatureTile->effect.tile.flags & IS_PLAYER) ||
        (attackedCreatureTile->effect.tile.flags & IS_PLAYER))
      puts("missed!");
  }
}
```

The defeat_creature() function is now needed before the above code will compile. This function makes a random check and if success it creates an item type to drop onto the base tile that previously contained the defeated creature. Specifically the code will transform the SpriteTile of the creature into a tile with flags IS_ITEM. The item will be of a random type and be appended to the terrain base tile list.

The defeat_creature() function is created below, please read and follow along with the source code logic to support awarding experience and dropping items.

```
/*...................................................................*/
/* defeat_creature: Player has defeated a creature                   */
/*                                                                   */
/*   Input: creatureTile is pointer to attacking creature/sprite     */
/*          attackedCreatureTile is the creature being attacked      */
/*...................................................................*/
static void defeat_creature(PlayerTile *characterTile,
                            SpriteTile *attackedCreatureTile)
{
  Tile *currentTile;
  u32 d16roll;

  // Increase character experience
  characterTile->player.currentWorld->score += 1;

  // Roll 16 sided dice
  d16roll = rand() % 16;

  // Check if an item is dropped (little more than third)
  if (d16roll > 5)
  {
    puts("Treasure dropped!");

    // Drop a random item

    // Re-roll, equipment is 0 through 15
    d16roll = (rand() % 16);

    //Give out potions most often
    if (d16roll < 8)
      d16roll = 0;

    // Re-role and morph roll to denzi_data.h
    else if ((d16roll = (rand() % 16)) == 4)
      d16roll += 1;
    else if (d16roll == 5)
```

```
  d16roll += 2;
else  if (d16roll == 6)
  d16roll = ITEM_HELMET;
else if (d16roll == 7)
  d16roll = ITEM_CHAINMAIL;
else if (d16roll >= 8)
{
  // Do not release rare items until fifth level
  if (characterTile->player.currentWorld->score <= 5)
  {
    d16roll -= 8;
  }
  else
  {
    // Reduce top four items until 10th level
    if ((characterTile->player.currentWorld->score < 10) &&
        (d16roll > 8 + 3))
      d16roll -= 4;

    // Assign the tile item to replace the die roll
    if (d16roll == 8)
      d16roll = ITEM_BATTLEAXE;
    else if (d16roll == 9)
      d16roll = ITEM_PLATEMAIL;
    else if (d16roll == 10)
      d16roll = ITEM_SPLINTMAIL;
    else if (d16roll == 11)
      d16roll = ITEM_MAGIC_BELT;
    else if (d16roll == 12)
      d16roll = ITEM_POWER_STAFF;
    else if (d16roll == 13)
      d16roll = ITEM_FLAMING_SWORD;
    else if (d16roll == 14)
      d16roll = ITEM_LIGHTNING_SWORD;
    else if (d16roll == 15)
      d16roll = ITEM_POWER_SWORD;
```

```
      }
    }

    // Convert defeated creature into equipment item on terrain
    attackedCreatureTile->effect.tile.color = COLOR_WHITE;
    attackedCreatureTile->effect.tile.tileNum = d16roll;
    attackedCreatureTile->effect.tile.bitmap = EquipmentData;
    attackedCreatureTile->effect.tile.flags = IS_ITEM | IS_VISIBLE;
    attackedCreatureTile->effect.tile.list.previous = NULL;
    attackedCreatureTile->effect.tile.list.next = NULL;

    // Add to the end of the list
    currentTile = GameGridTile(attackedCreatureTile->effect.locationX,
                              attackedCreatureTile->effect.locationY);
    if (currentTile)
      ListAppend(attackedCreatureTile, currentTile);

    // Display dropped item tile using attackedCreatureTile's tile
    TileDisplayScreen((Tile *)attackedCreatureTile, GAME_GRID_START_X +
                (attackedCreatureTile->effect.locationX * TILE_WIDTH),
              GAME_GRID_START_Y +
              (attackedCreatureTile->effect.locationY * TILE_HEIGHT));
  }
  puts("Creature defeated!");

  // Update XP on display
  player_display(&TheCharacter);
}
```

12.4 Sprite Behavior

The combination of creature detection and behavior (pursue, retreat, ignore, etc.), applied with terrain that is impassable and a random generated map will result in a game experience that is unique per game level. This dynamic feel, where each game and level is different, is an important ingredient for creating a compelling game. To make the game even more dynamic requires an intelligent world, that is both believable and unique.

Informed decision making is one of the baselines for intelligence. Let us review the behavior flags from last chapter for sprites again. A 'cautious' behavior will flee from stronger creatures, 'aggressive' will pursue, 'ambush' will hide and attack any creature that wanders into range, 'vision' means the creature has exceptional vision and can see a few game grid tiles away. 'Tracking' means the creature can track and can thus see/identify creatures even further away. 'Flying' and 'is dead' identify creatures that can fly or who have been previously defeated.

```
// Creature flags
#define AGGRESSIVE          (1 << 0)
#define AMBUSH              (1 << 1)
#define CAUTIOUS            (1 << 2)
#define VISION              (1 << 3)
#define TRACKING            (1 << 4)
#define FLYING              (1 << 5)
#define IS_DEAD             (1 << 7)
```

Informed decisions are the base of intelligence for sprites in this game. The sprite logic will also need to identify surrounding terrain and creatures to make an informed decision on when and where to act, such as to move, hide or attack. If we extend the decisions of creatures from "flee and hide" to "hide and ambush" we can make their behavior less reactionary and more life like and surprising to encounter for the player.

The predefined decisions for creatures are not true intelligence, nor will their consistent application engage players for long. One improvement is to introduce better decision making to the "pursue" behavior algorithm, so that the creature can look ahead at the terrain and choose the best of multiple paths to intercept the creature being pursued. This decision making can be applied to the creatures statistics as well, for example the pursue and flee behaviors of a creature can depend on how powerful the detected creature is. So the creature pursues weaker creatures, ignores creatures of it's own type, and flees from creatures more powerful.

12.5 Sprite Actions

Now we will create a world where the creatures scattered over the country side can be a diverse ecosystem, some hunting, hiding or sneaking among themselves, with the player character entering with courage and attention. To accomplish this we start with sprite_action(), which performs an action for a sprite (move, attack, hide, etc.) based on the behavior of the creature (aggressive, etc.) and if any other creatures are nearby. The final function needed for **actions** is sprite_find_nearest(), which will search the nearby game grid and return the nearest creature in range (if any) so that sprite_action() can make an informed decision.

```
/*.................................................................*/
/* sprite_action: Perform an action for a sprite                   */
/*                                                                 */
/*   Input: creatureTile is pointer to creature sprite to act      */
/*          nearestCreatureTile the sprite nearest on game grid    */
/*                                                                 */
/*  Return: TRUE (1) if action performed, FALSE (0) if no action   */
/*.................................................................*/
static int sprite_action(SpriteTile *creatureTile,
                         SpriteTile *nearestCreatureTile)
{
  Tile *theTerrain;
  ActionTile *attack = attack_range(creatureTile, nearestCreatureTile);
  int x, y;

  // Allow creatures to hide in towns
  theTerrain = creatureTile->currentWorld->tiles;
  if (theTerrain[nearestCreatureTile->effect.locationX +
          (nearestCreatureTile->effect.locationY * GAME_GRID_WIDTH)].
                                          tileNum == STRUCTURE_TOWN)
    return FALSE;

  // Determine x offset toward distantCreature
  if (creatureTile->effect.locationX <
```

```
    nearestCreatureTile->effect.locationX)
  x = 1;
else if (creatureTile->effect.locationX ==
         nearestCreatureTile->effect.locationX)
  x = 0;
else
  x = -1;

// Determine y offset toward distantCreature
if (creatureTile->effect.locationY <
    nearestCreatureTile->effect.locationY)
  y = 1;
else if (creatureTile->effect.locationY ==
         nearestCreatureTile->effect.locationY)
  y = 0;
else
  y = -1;

// If creature is aggressive, attack or pursue
if (creatureTile->stats.flags & AGGRESSIVE)
{
  if (attack)
    creature_attack(creatureTile, attack, nearestCreatureTile);
  else
    sprite_move(creatureTile, creatureTile->effect.locationX + x,
                creatureTile->effect.locationY + y);
  return TRUE;
}

// Otherwise if cautious, attack if in range or move away
else if (creatureTile->stats.flags & CAUTIOUS)
{
  if (attack)
    creature_attack(creatureTile, attack, nearestCreatureTile);
  else
    sprite_move(creatureTile, creatureTile->effect.locationX - x,
```

```
                  creatureTile->effect.locationY - y);
    return TRUE;
  }

  // Otherwise act as undetected (ignore the nearby creature)
  return FALSE;
}

/*...................................................................*/
/* sprite_find_nearest: Find the nearest sprite on game grid        */
/*                                                                   */
/*   Input: creatureTile is pointer to creature to search nearby     */
/*                                                                   */
/*  Return: Pointer to the nearest SpriteTile, or NULL               */
/*...................................................................*/
static SpriteTile *sprite_find_nearest(SpriteTile *creatureTile)
{
  int x, y, distance, startX, startY, endX, endY, curr_distance;
  Tile *theTerrain;

  // Determine distance creature can perceive
  if (creatureTile->stats.flags & TRACKING)
    distance = 5;
  else if (creatureTile->stats.flags & VISION)
    distance = 3;
  else
    distance = 1;

  // Check in concentric rings around the sprite
  for (curr_distance = 1; curr_distance <= distance; ++curr_distance)
  {
    startX = creatureTile->effect.locationX - curr_distance;
    if (startX < 0)
      startX = 0;
    endX = creatureTile->effect.locationX + curr_distance;
    if (endX >= GAME_GRID_WIDTH)
```

```
      endX = GAME_GRID_WIDTH - 1;

    startY = creatureTile->effect.locationY - curr_distance;
    if (startY < 0)
      startY = 0;
    endY = creatureTile->effect.locationY + curr_distance;
    if (endY >= GAME_GRID_HEIGHT)
      endY = GAME_GRID_HEIGHT - 1;

    for (y = startY; y <= endY; ++y)
    {
      for (x = startX; x <= endX; ++x)
      {
        // Find the specific terrain tile for this location
        theTerrain = creatureTile->currentWorld->tiles;
        theTerrain = &(theTerrain[x + y * GAME_GRID_WIDTH]);

        // Check terrain tile for creatures (sprite)
        if (theTerrain->list.next)
        {
          Tile *stackedTile;

          for (stackedTile = (void *)theTerrain->list.next;
               stackedTile; stackedTile = (void *)stackedTile->list.next)
          {
            if ((stackedTile != (Tile *)creatureTile) &&
                (stackedTile->flags & IS_VISIBLE) &&
                (stackedTile->flags & (IS_CREATURE | IS_PLAYER)))
              return (SpriteTile *)stackedTile;
          }
        }
      }
    }
  }

  // Return no nearby creature
```

```
  return NULL;
}
```

12.6 Game Flow

Vital to the game flow is also the code to move the player. It must check that the move is valid and then look around as well as pick up any item (IS_ITEM flag) in the tile list. Specifically if an item is on the list and the player does not yet have the item it is automatically picked up and utilized by the player. Depending on the type of item, and player class, the item may increase the players attack(s), armour class or hit points. Different classes have different rules on the items they can utilize. All classes can use leather armour, but wizards cannot use shields, scouts and wizards cannot use heavy armour and clerics and wizards cannot use bow and arrows. Finally, only wizards can use the power staff and clerics the lightning sword. After checking for level up in player_move() add this code to pick up any item tiles and improve the players situation. This code should be added after checking for the WORLD_EXIT flag and leveling up.

```
...
    // Character picks up any item if room
    if (destinationTerrain->list.next &&
        (destinationTerrain->list.next != (void *)destinationTerrain)&&
        (characterTile->num_items <= MAX_ITEMS))
    {
      int i;
      Tile *stackedTile;

      // Find the item within the tile list
      for (stackedTile = (void *)destinationTerrain->list.next;
           stackedTile && (stackedTile != destinationTerrain) &&
           !(stackedTile->flags & IS_ITEM);
           stackedTile = (void *)stackedTile->list.next) ;

      // If an item was found (NULL ending or circular) get it
      if ((stackedTile) && (stackedTile != destinationTerrain))
```

```
{
  puts("Item located");

  // Ignore duplicate items
  for (i = 0; i < characterTile->num_items; ++i)
  {
    if (characterTile->items[i].tileNum ==
                                      stackedTile->tileNum)
      break;
  }

  // If not a duplicate item, add it to the character
  if (i == characterTile->num_items)
  {
    if (stackedTile->tileNum == ITEM_POTION)
    {
      // Drink right away
      characterTile->player.stats.hp += 8;
      puts("The potion energizes you.");
    }
    else
    {
      if (stackedTile->tileNum == ITEM_ARMOUR_LEATHER)
        characterTile->player.stats.ac += 1;

      else if (!(characterTile->player.stats.flags &
                                                CLASS_WIZARD))
      {
        if (stackedTile->tileNum == ITEM_ARMOUR_SHEILD)
          characterTile->player.stats.ac += 2;

        if (!(characterTile->player.stats.flags & CLASS_SCOUT))
        {
          if (stackedTile->tileNum == ITEM_PLATEMAIL)
            characterTile->player.stats.ac = 18;
          else if (stackedTile->tileNum == ITEM_SPLINTMAIL)
```

```
      characterTile->player.stats.ac = 17;
    else if (stackedTile->tileNum == ITEM_CHAINMAIL)
      characterTile->player.stats.ac = 16;
    else if (stackedTile->tileNum == ITEM_GAUNTLETS)
      characterTile->player.stats.ac += 1;
  }

  if (stackedTile->tileNum == ITEM_WEAPON_SWORD)
  {
    characterTile->player.stats.first.affect += 1;
    characterTile->player.stats.first.effect.tile.tileNum =
                                              ITEM_WEAPON_SWORD;
  }
  else if (stackedTile->tileNum == ITEM_FLAMING_SWORD)
  {
    characterTile->player.stats.first.affect += 1;
    characterTile->player.stats.first.effect.tile.tileNum =
                                             ITEM_FLAMING_SWORD;
  }
  else if (stackedTile->tileNum == ITEM_POWER_SWORD)
  {
    characterTile->player.stats.first.affect += 1;
    if (characterTile->player.stats.str >= 16)
      characterTile->player.stats.str += 3;
    else
      characterTile->player.stats.str = 18;
   characterTile->player.stats.first.effect.tile.tileNum =
                                               ITEM_POWER_SWORD;
}

  if (!(characterTile->player.stats.flags &
                         (CLASS_CLERIC | CLASS_WIZARD)))
  {
    if (stackedTile->tileNum == ITEM_WEAPON_BOW)
    {
      characterTile->player.stats.second.affect += 1;
```

```
        characterTile->player.stats.second.range = 3;
        characterTile->player.stats.second.name = "zing";
      }
    }
  }
  else
  {
    if (stackedTile->tileNum == ITEM_POWER_STAFF)
    {
      characterTile->player.stats.first.affect += 2;
      characterTile->player.stats.first.effect.tile.tileNum =
                                            ITEM_POWER_STAFF;
      characterTile->player.stats.second.affect += 1;
        characterTile->player.stats.second.range += 2;
      characterTile->player.stats.second.effect.tile.tileNum=
                                                   ITEM_BALL;
    }
  }

  if (stackedTile->tileNum == ITEM_HELMET)
    characterTile->player.stats.ac += 1;
  else if (stackedTile->tileNum == ITEM_LIGHTNING_SWORD)
  {
    if (characterTile->player.stats.flags & CLASS_CLERIC)
    {
      characterTile->player.stats.first.affect += 2;
      characterTile->player.stats.first.effect.tile.tileNum =
                                            ITEM_POWER_STAFF;
      characterTile->player.stats.second.affect += 1;
      characterTile->player.stats.second.range += 2;
      characterTile->player.stats.second.effect.tile.tileNum=
                                                   ITEM_BALL;
    }
  }

  characterTile->items[characterTile->num_items++] =
```

```
                                                        *stackedTile;
            puts("Item taken");
          }

          player_display(characterTile);

          // Remove the item from the background tile
          ListRemove(stackedTile->list);
        }
      }
...
```

12.7 Sprite Randomness

The final function needed before we can bring the sprites to life is the sprite_move_-random() function. This function uses **randomness** to move a **sprite** in a random direction one **tile** on the **game grid**. The 'randX' and 'randY' variables are randomly generated and if both are zero then the creature does not move. By checking if the last bit is less than 8 ((random & 0x0F) < 8) we use more **randomness** and get a better averaged random result vs. if we only checked the last bit (random & 1).

Note in the algorithm below we introduce the inline C conditional statement. Simple C if statements can be written as an expression using the (expression) ? statementTrue : statementFalse syntax. The expression before the question (?) is the if (expression) and the statement after the question (?) is evaluated if the expression is true. If the expression is not true, the statement after the colon (:) is evaluated. So '((random & 0x0F) < 8) ? 1 : 0' evaluates to 1 if the nibble is less than 8, or zero (0) if not. The code effectively averages 8 bits of randomness into a zero or one.

The final function, sprite_move_random(), can be used by sprites when no nearby creature is detected and the creature is hunting or otherwise wandering across the countryside.

```
/*.....................................................................*/
/* sprite_move_random: Move sprite one tile in random direction        */
/*                                                                     */
/*   Input: creatureTile is pointer to creature sprite to move         */
/*.....................................................................*/
static void sprite_move_random(SpriteTile *creatureTile)
{
  int random, randX, randY;

  // If creature is out of bounds (or dead) do not move
  if ((creatureTile->effect.locationX < 0) ||
      (creatureTile->effect.locationY < 0) ||
      (creatureTile->stats.flags & IS_DEAD) ||
      (creatureTile->stats.hp <= 0))
    return;

  // Generate randX and randY bits, zero or one
  random = rand();
  randX = ((random & 0x0F) < 8) ? 1 : 0;
  if (random < 0)
    randX = -randX;

  random = rand();
  randY = ((random & 0x0F) < 8) ? 1 : 0;
  if (random < 0)
    randY = -randY;

  // Move the creature randomly
  if (randX || randY)
  {
    if ((creatureTile->effect.locationX + randX >
         (GAME_GRID_WIDTH - 1)) ||
        (creatureTile->effect.locationX + randX < 0))
      randX = -randX;

    if ((creatureTile->effect.locationY + randY >
```

```
          (GAME_GRID_HEIGHT - 1)) ||
         (creatureTile->effect.locationY + randY < 0))
      randY = -randY;

    sprite_move(creatureTile, creatureTile->effect.locationX + randX,
                creatureTile->effect.locationY + randY);
  }
}
```

It is also possible to introduce weather, represented using EffectTiles with a wind direction and duration. Then EffectTiles would algorithmically drift over the world differently as the EffectTiles move through different base terrain Tiles. This type of virtual world could be used to simulate weather patters upon natural worlds and not be a 'game' at all. We will leave it to the reader to create such a world.

12.8 Game Rounds

Now that we that we have all the sprite primitives in place, such as movements and **actions** let us combine it all together to create the virtual world game logic. The glue is a scheduled timer callback game_round() function that binds everything together. The game round callback should, for every creature sprite in the game, search for nearby creatures and perform a creature specific and appropriate sprite action for that game round, such as pursue, flee, attack, hide or random wander.

Let us read through the game_round() function source code now and identify the creature behavior and decision making process.

```
/*...........................................................*/
/* game_round: Timer callback to perform round of sprite actions    */
/*                                                                  */
/*   Input: unused is an unused parameter                           */
/*          character is void pointer to PlayerTile                 */
/*          creatures is void pointer to array of CreatureTile's    */
/*                                                                  */
/*  Return: TASK_FINISHED                                           */
/*...........................................................*/
```

```
static int game_round(u32 unused, void *character, void *creatures)
{
  static int lastX = 0, lastY = 0, maxHp = 0;
  SpriteTile *creatureTiles = creatures;
  PlayerTile *characterTile = character;
  SpriteTile *nearbyCreature;
  int i;

  putchar('+');
  StdioState = &ConsoleState;

  // Perform an action for the creatures
  for (i = 0; i < characterTile->player.currentWorld->level + 1; ++i)
  {
    if (!(creatureTiles[i].effect.tile.flags & IS_DEAD))
    {
      if (creatureTiles[i].stats.hp > 0)
      {
        // Check if there are any nearby creatures
        nearbyCreature = sprite_find_nearest(&creatureTiles[i]);

        // If no nearby creature or no action, have creature wander
        if (!(nearbyCreature &&
              sprite_action(&creatureTiles[i], nearbyCreature)))
        {
          if (creatureTiles[i].stats.flags & AMBUSH)
          {
            // If we have not moved for three rounds, hide
            if (creatureTiles[i].stats.scratch >= 3)
            {
              creatureTiles[i].effect.tile.flags &= ~IS_VISIBLE;

              // Redraw tile after sprite hid
              TileDisplayGrid(creatureTiles[i].effect.locationX,
                              creatureTiles[i].effect.locationY);
            }
```

```
          else if (creatureTiles[i].effect.tile.flags & IS_VISIBLE)
            ++creatureTiles[i].stats.scratch;
        }
        else
          sprite_move_random(&creatureTiles[i]);
      }
    }
    else
      creatureTiles[i].effect.tile.flags |= IS_DEAD;
  }
}

...
```

While rounds strictly control creature sprites it is also necessary to capture some player logic within the game rounds. If the player has not moved or attacked for some number of rounds the player may hide (if scout) or heal itself (if cleric). We also check if the player died within the previous game round and end the game if so.

```
...
  // Perform an action for the character
  if (characterTile)
  {
    // The character must be conscious to act
    if (characterTile->player.stats.hp > 0)
    {
      // If cleric, check to see if no movement long enough to heal
      if (characterTile->player.stats.flags & CLASS_CLERIC)
      {
        if (characterTile->player.stats.hp > maxHp)
          maxHp = characterTile->player.stats.hp;

        if ((lastX == characterTile->player.effect.locationX) &&
            (lastY == characterTile->player.effect.locationY))
          ++creatureTiles[i].stats.scratch;
        else
```

```
    creatureTiles[i].stats.scratch = 0;

  if ((characterTile->player.stats.hp < maxHp) &&
      (creatureTiles[i].stats.scratch > 4))
  {
    // Roll healing and add proficiency
    int hp = (rand() % 8) + 2 +
             (characterTile->player.currentWorld->score >> 4);

    // Add wisdom modifier
    if (characterTile->player.stats.wis > 10)
      hp += (characterTile->player.stats.wis - 10) >> 1;

    if (hp + characterTile->player.stats.hp < maxHp)
      characterTile->player.stats.hp += hp;
    else
      characterTile->player.stats.hp = maxHp;

    putbyte(hp);
    puts("You are healed");
    creatureTiles[i].stats.scratch = 0;
    player_display(characterTile);
  }

  lastX = characterTile->player.effect.locationX;
  lastY = characterTile->player.effect.locationY;
}

// If scout check to see if we stay still long enough to hide
else if (characterTile->player.stats.flags & CLASS_SCOUT)
{
  if ((lastX == characterTile->player.effect.locationX) &&
      (lastY == characterTile->player.effect.locationY))
    ++characterTile->player.stats.scratch;
  else
  {
```

```
          characterTile->player.stats.scratch = 0;
          characterTile->player.effect.tile.flags |= IS_VISIBLE;
        }
        if (characterTile->player.stats.scratch > 3)
        {
          if (characterTile->player.effect.tile.flags & IS_VISIBLE)
            puts("Hiding");
          characterTile->player.effect.tile.flags &= ~IS_VISIBLE;
        }

        lastX = characterTile->player.effect.locationX;
        lastY = characterTile->player.effect.locationY;
      }
    }
    else
    {
      puts("You died, game over");
      TimerCancel(TheWorld.round);
      TheWorld.round = NULL;
      return TASK_FINISHED;
    }
  }

  // Schedule next game round and return finished
  TheWorld.round = TimerSchedule(TheWorld.period, game_round,
                                 &TheCharacter, TheCreatures);
  return TASK_FINISHED;
}
```

That is it, the game is now ready to play! Congratulations on getting this far and thank you for completing this journey to learn how to create system software. Don't forget to personalize the game and make it better with your own changes now that you have experience creating system software.